UNCOVER THE ROOTS
of Challenging Behavior

"This book is a must-have for all early education professionals! It is an accessible, comprehensive primer for those new to the field, giving you a wealth of both proactive and reactive strategies and resources that will create a successful, thriving community of young learners. Experienced educators will also find the book solidly grounded in well-established theory and research but written with a fresh voice that will provoke your thinking, provide new ideas, and add value to your classroom practices. If you follow Ms. Salcedo's sound advice, your 'garden' of seedlings will surely blossom and grow. Highly recommend!"

—**Richard Cohen, M.A.,** international early education motivational speaker and consultant

"All teachers struggle with behavior issues that perplex them—what to do when Johnny won't sit at circle time, when Meg lashes out, when Enrique keeps disturbing his classmates. *But what if we could create classroom environments that help prevent these behaviors from happening in the first place?* With this important book, early childhood expert Michelle Salcedo offers specific, carefully considered, research-based strategies and ideas that will make your classroom as effective, responsive, and joyful as possible . . . an abundant garden of blooming possibilities!"

—**Diane Ohanesian,** early childhood development specialist, former editor-in-chief of *Early Childhood Today*, and author of *Hugga Bugga Love*

"Early care professionals spend an exorbitant amount of time brainstorming appropriate responses to inappropriate behaviors displayed in the classroom. *Uncover the Roots of Challenging Behavior* is an excellent tool that can be used to support the paradigm shift from reactive to proactive classroom guidance. Michelle Salcedo captures the transition from theory to practice by identifying essential components needed to support students through a vulnerable stage of development. Teachers walk away with specific strategies that can be immediately used in the classroom."

—**Sheila Lewis, Ed.D.,** early childhood educator

"*Uncover the Roots of Challenging Behavior* is one of those books that will be looked at frequently. It does a marvelous job simplifying why challenging behaviors occur and the best ways to prevent them. Informative and engaging, the ideas can be used immediately. Everyone should keep this book where you can pull it out for a quick solution."

—**Daniel Hodgins,** author of *Boys: Changing the Classroom, Not the Child* and *Get Over It! Relearning Guidance Practices*

"Helping young children develop into socially competent and caring adults starts early. In *Uncover the Roots of Challenging Behavior*, Michelle Salcedo provides a wealth of information for teachers at all levels. She includes strategies for establishing the classroom environment and effective guidance techniques for teachers to try in their own classrooms. Teachers will find her ideas, charts, and stories helpful for not only critically examining their own behavior, but also working to develop the key relationships and appropriate learning settings that truly help children thrive."

—**Karen Menke Paciorek, Ph.D.**, professor, Early Childhood Education & Children and Families at Eastern Michigan University

"If you are seeking practical, specific, and supportive ways to create classroom environments, step right this way. In *Uncover the Roots of Challenging Behavior*, Michelle Salcedo reminds us behavior is a powerful form of communication. She provides practical suggestions and concrete examples on how to create classroom environments that support educators in hearing this communication and meeting the often unmet needs of children."

—**Brigid Beaubien, Ph.D.**, professor, Teacher Education, Eastern Michigan University

"This book offers a variety of ways to address challenging behavior: analyzing your environment, evaluating your schedule and materials, and offering suggestions about how you build relationships with children in your care. Most importantly, Michelle Salcedo encourages us to ask the question, 'What are children telling us with their behavior?' As you uncover the answers to that question, you can help find ways to ensure each child feels safe, valued, and heard."

—**Sandra Heidemann, M.S.**, coauthor of *The Thinking Teacher: A Framework for Intentional Teaching in the Early Childhood Classroom*

UNCOVER THE ROOTS
of Challenging Behavior

Create Responsive Environments
Where Young Children Thrive

Michelle Salcedo, M.Ed.

free spirit
PUBLISHING®

Library of Congress Cataloging-in-Publication Data

Names: Salcedo, Michelle, 1966– author.

Title: Uncover the roots of challenging behavior : create responsive environments where young children thrive / by Michelle Salcedo.

Description: Minneapolis, MN : Free Spirit Publishing, [2018] | Includes bibliographical references and index. | Description based on print version record and CIP data provided by publisher; resource not viewed.

Identifiers: LCCN 2017045640 (print) | LCCN 2018016425 (ebook) | ISBN 9781631982880 (Web PDF) | ISBN 9781631982897 (ePub) | ISBN 9781631981753 (pbk.) | ISBN 1631981757 (pbk.)

Subjects: LCSH: Early childhood education. | Problem children—Education (Early childhood) | Problem children—Behavior modification. | Behavior modification. | Educational psychology.

Classification: LCC LB1139.23 (ebook) | LCC LB1139.23 .S248 2018 (print) | DDC 372.21—dc23

LC record available at https://lccn.loc.gov/2017045640

Free Spirit Publishing does not have control over or assume responsibility for author or third-party websites and their content. At the time of this book's publication, all facts and figures cited within are the most current available. All telephone numbers, addresses, and website URLs are accurate and active; all publications, organizations, websites, and other resources exist as described in this book; and all have been verified as of September 2021. If you find an error or believe that a resource listed here is not as described, please contact Free Spirit Publishing. Parents, teachers, and other adults: We strongly urge you to monitor children's use of the internet.

Parts of this book were adapted from "Classrooms as the Root of Challenging Behaviors" by Michelle Salcedo (*Exchange*, January/February 2015) and "Are Your Children in Times Square?" by Sandra Duncan and Michelle Salcedo (*Exchange*, September/October 2016). Used with permission.

Parts of this book previously appeared in a training session on challenging behavior that the author created for Quorum Learning, operated by Quality Assist. Content is used with permission. For more information, visit quorumlearning.com.

Parts of this book also have appeared on the website, on the blog, and in printed materials that the author created for the Sunshine House, Inc. Content is used with permission.

Note: The names of teachers and children who appear in this book have been changed to protect their privacy.

Edited by Meg Bratsch
Cover and interior design by Emily Dyer

Photo credits: Cover © Monkey Business Images | Dreamstime.com; © Andreykuzmin | Dreamstime.com; p. 9 © Vitmark | Dreamstime.com; p. 11 © Jowita Dusza | Dreamstime.com; p. 50 © Sattva78 | Dreamstime.com; pp. 51, 67, 108, 109, 131 © Monkey Business Images | Dreamstime.com; p. 66 © Warangkana Charuyodhin | Dreamstime.com; p. 75 © Parinyabinsuk | Dreamstime.com; p. 77 © Darko64 | Dreamstime.com; p. 103 © Zlikovec | Dreamstime.com; p. 124 © Petro | Dreamstime.com; pp. 125, 152 © Rawpixelimages | Dreamstime.com; p. 133 © YaoRusheng | Dreamstime.com; p. 144 © Oksun70 | Dreamstime.com

Printed in China

Free Spirit Publishing
An imprint of Teacher Created Materials
9850 51st Avenue North, Suite 100
Minneapolis, MN 55442
(612) 338-2068
help4kids@freespirit.com
freespirit.com

Dedication

To my friends and family, near and far, of blood and of heart. You know what you've done and you know who you are. Thank you for being in my life.

Especially to Nacho, Christian, and Sheridan—my rocks of endless love and support.

Acknowledgments

Many influences have shaped my professional journey and ultimately have led to this book. It would be impossible to thank everyone, but please know that I hold you all dear.

Thank you to Bill Weld-Wallis, who many years ago invited me into this realm of early childhood education.

Thank you to Richard Cohen and Deb Moss. I am the professional I am today because of the time I spent with both of you. Your guidance and encouragement opened up to me a whole new world of early childhood.

Thank you to Sandra Duncan, who helped me discover this enchanting world of early childhood writing and who has been one of my most ardent advocates ever since. Thank you for putting your support and wisdom into writing the foreword to this book.

Thanks to my editor, Meg Bratsch. You got me into this, and you have managed to get me through the process with grace and patience. This book is so much better because of your influence.

Thanks especially to all the early childhood professionals who, every day, care for and educate our children. I know that the world will be a better place tomorrow because of the work you do today.

Thanks to my parents, Art and Joan, who taught me that it is possible to live in accordance with one's principles.

Finally, I would like to thank the children. You fill the world with joy, laughter, and energy—thank you for letting me be part of your world, even for a moment at a time.

Contents

List of Figures

List of Reproducible Forms

See page 178 for instructions for downloading digital forms.

Foreword

Who doesn't love receiving gifts? My mom's favorite gift was fresh flowers, especially pink roses—so naturally that was my dad's go-to present for her birthday, their anniversary, or Valentine's Day. On one special occasion, my dad veered away from the standard gift of fresh flowers and surprised her with a small rose bush, which he carefully planted beside the back door of the house. Mom was thrilled and delighted with the bush of tiny pink roses. Unfortunately, the little rose bush didn't make it past the second growing season. Although dismayed, Mom decided to learn all she could about growing roses. She read books, talked with neighbors, and visited the local nursery. A transformation slowly took place: She became *more* than a lover of roses—Mom became a gardener. She found a better spot in the yard with more sun, prepared the soil, and provided the right nutrients. Although it was challenging, she worked hard . . . and the result was healthy, thriving rose bushes filled with gorgeous and grandiose roses. For the roses to thrive, Mom learned it is important to fix the environment in which the roses grow—and not the roses themselves.

The book you are holding in your hands encourages you to follow in my mom's footsteps: Become a gardener. As you work with young children—especially those exhibiting challenging behaviors—begin by making changes in the classroom environment rather than focusing on or trying to fix the children. Understand classroom factors that can contribute to challenging behaviors and learn strategies to reduce the likelihood children will act out in your classroom. Learn how you can create learning spaces responsive to the developmental needs of young children. Be proactive and not reactive. Discover a comprehensive approach to fixing the classroom environment to prevent and address young children's challenging behaviors.

Just like my mom, you can be a superb gardener—only your garden is the classroom and your roses are the children. *Uncover the Roots of Challenging Behavior: Create Responsive Environments Where Young Children Thrive* is a groundbreaking perspective on understanding how classroom environments impact children's behaviors. This powerful book offers many proactive strategies you can use to reduce challenging behaviors simply by changing the classroom environment. By telling real-world stories based on her vast experiences working with young children, author Michelle Salcedo illustrates compelling and thought-provoking ideas and valuable concepts. Packed with easy-to-understand and ready-to-use tips and advice, this book is bound to become a favorite and treasured resource for all early childhood gardeners.

Sandra Duncan, Ed.D., early childhood educator and coauthor of *Bringing the Outside In* and *Inspiring Spaces for Young Children*

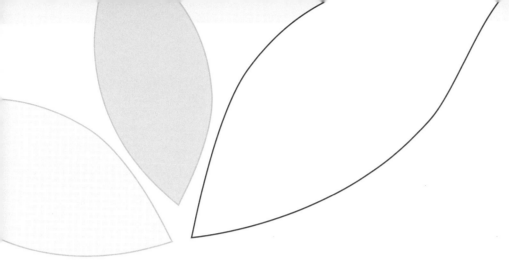

Introduction

In the early 2000s, I served as the lead teacher and training director of a small nonprofit early learning center in northwest Detroit. A determined executive director had recruited me with the words, "These children need you, Michelle." Over the years, the center had become a final refuge for children who had been expelled from other facilities due to challenging behaviors. The director didn't know how to support these children, but she firmly believed that they were too young for the world to give up on them. So there I was, in a classroom with twenty-five children, age two-and-a-half to five, many of whom had been removed from at least two other programs before passing through our doors. What I saw were very young kids who were trying to make sense of their worlds. For many, the circumstances of their current lives made it very difficult to be in a learning center environment. The structures and expectations of a toddler or preschool classroom were too much for them, so they lashed out with problem behaviors that signaled their frustrations or feelings of inadequacy.

The scenes I saw every day may feel familiar to you, as an early childhood educator:

> *A boy, angry because he doesn't want to clean up, picks up a chair and throws it across the room.*

> *A girl, resistant to taking a nap, begins hitting other children lying peacefully on their cots.*

> *A preschooler, frustrated with the expectations of circle time, runs around the classroom, screaming and pushing over shelves.*

In early childhood classrooms across North America, situations like these play out repeatedly. Teachers become increasingly frustrated as they struggle to help children with challenging behaviors integrate into the classroom community while fearing for the physical and emotional well-being of the other children.

Most teachers choose the field of early childhood education because they want to make a difference in children's lives. However, many report that they feel unequipped to handle instances like those just described. Teachers are often overwhelmed and feel helpless in the face of these challenging behaviors. Families are frustrated, are embarrassed, and may feel judged for not being able to "fix" their children. Directors, trying to balance the needs of an individual child with those of their staff and the other children, may resort to expelling a misbehaving child from their programs.

There is increasing focus on the rate at which our youngest learners are being expelled from preschool programs.[1] Some reports show that nearly seven out of every thousand children are expelled at least once from a preK classroom. This is more than three times the rate for higher grades.[2] And data show that these expulsions impact boys, especially minority boys, at a much higher rate than girls.[3] These numbers solely reflect children in preK programs in public schools. When we take into account the myriad other programs and add in the number of children who are asked to leave schools even before the age of four, the statistics are likely even more dramatic.

Politicians and experts argue about the causes of these alarming numbers. Institutions blame families, and families point the finger at institutions. While policy makers debate on how to address the issue of expulsion in the early years, teachers are left to support the diverse needs of the children in their classrooms—including those who exhibit challenging behaviors. Most agree that kicking a child out of a program does nothing to actually address the underlying issues. That course of action only serves to move a vulnerable child and family out of one institution and often into another that is equally unequipped to deal with the challenges.

The Pyramid Model

As a teacher faced daily with addressing the many different needs of these children, I reached out for resources I could use to help them succeed. As part of my research, I spent a few days at a training institute on challenging behavior sponsored by the Center on the Social and Emotional Foundations for Early Learning (CSEFEL). What a relief it was to know I was not the only one struggling with these issues! I found myself amidst a whole community of people dedicated to understanding and dealing with young children's challenging behaviors.

At the CSEFEL, I was introduced to the Pyramid Model for Supporting Social-Emotional Competence in Infants and Young Children. It is this model that changed the way I looked at challenging behaviors and shaped the approaches you will read about in this book. The pyramid in **figure 1** shows us that children's behaviors do not happen in a vacuum. There are layers upon layers of systems and structures that, when put in place, can support children's learning and development so challenging behaviors are less likely to occur.[4]

The **dark-green section** of the pyramid tells us that many challenging behaviors can be avoided by building early childhood classrooms around the dual constructs of high-quality supportive environments and nurturing and responsive relationships between adults and children, all delivered by a highly trained, effective workforce (**dark-brown section**). The National Association for the Education of Young Children (NAEYC) would classify these relationships and environments as "developmentally appropriate practice," or DAP. When we design such classrooms, we proactively address challenging behaviors by incorporating practices that help children be successful in an early childhood environment.

Figure 1 The Pyramid Model for Supporting Social-Emotional Competence in Infants and Young Children*

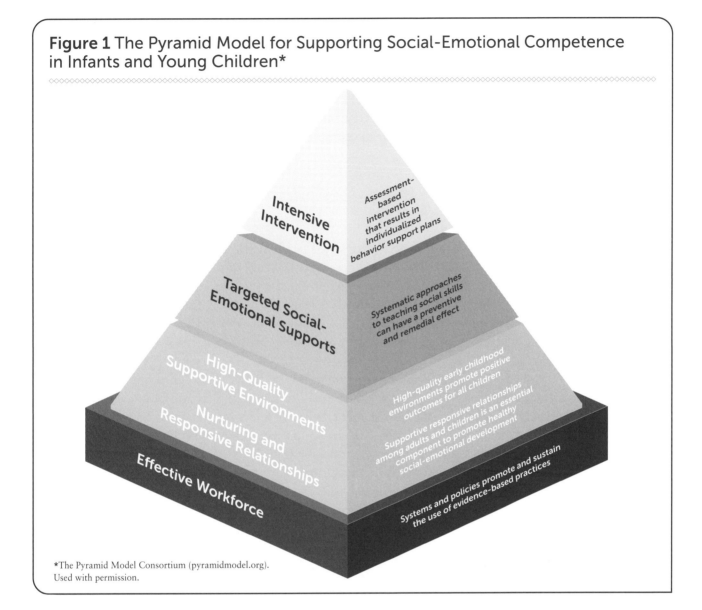

Intensive Intervention

Assessment-based intervention that results in individualized behavior support plans

Targeted Social-Emotional Supports

Systematic approaches to teaching social skills can have a preventive and remedial effect

High-Quality Supportive Environments

Nurturing and Responsive Relationships

High-quality early childhood environments promote positive outcomes for all children

Supportive responsive relationships among adults and children is an essential component to promote healthy social-emotional development

Effective Workforce

Systems and policies promote and sustain the use of evidence-based practices

*The Pyramid Model Consortium (pyramidmodel.org). Used with permission.

Even in the most developmentally appropriate classroom, however, challenging behaviors *will* occur. This is because children are learning about the world. They are learning their place in that world and how to live in it with other human beings. Hence, the **light-brown section** of the pyramid shows us that by creating consistent, instructive, and appropriate responses to challenging behaviors, we can help children learn social norms and expectations and make it less likely that the challenging behaviors will recur.

When all of these foundational structures are in place—a skilled workforce, nurturing relationships, a supportive environment, and targeted social-emotional responses—challenging behaviors are less likely to occur. When they do happen, children will learn from them and go on to meet expectations the next time.

And yet children will, at times, need additional supports in response to deeper factors that may be driving their behaviors. The top **green section** of the pyramid shows that these behaviors, while rare, call for more-intensive, intentional, and directed interactions.

Other programs, such as Response to Intervention (RTI) and Positive Behavioral Interventions and Supports (PBIS), have also advocated for a multilayered approach to addressing challenging behaviors in children. These programs rely on response-based methods in which interventions are focused on how providers respond to behaviors. Instead, the approaches in the Pyramid Model are proactive. They are designed around creating *environments* and *relationships* that support children's development so challenging behaviors are less likely to occur to begin with.

Behavior Is Communication

Children's behaviors, including those we see as challenging, are their attempts to communicate. When, as adults, we make a certain gesture to the driver who just cut us off, we are communicating our anger at our current situation. Children are just figuring out how to navigate this confusing world. They find themselves often frustrated, overwhelmed, or angry, with little ability to name—let alone express—those feelings in a constructive way. And so their behaviors speak for them.

Not only do young children lack the ability to vocalize their feelings, they are often at a loss for how to identify their needs, both emotional and physical. When teachers are dealing with challenging behaviors, it is important to first rule out physical causes for the behaviors. A child who is constantly knocking into other children, crowding others, or touching them without permission may be communicating that her vision is impaired. A visit to an eye doctor and a pair of glasses may fix the problem. A child who does not listen or speaks very loudly may be communicating that he is not hearing well. Instead of needing to learn to follow the rules, the child may need tubes in his ears or hearing aids. If a child is exhibiting challenging behaviors and a physical cause is suspected, a trip to the family healthcare provider is often the first step in discovering and resolving the underlying issue.

> Not only do young children lack the ability to vocalize their feelings, they are often at a loss for how to identify their needs.

Children's emotional needs are usually even more difficult for them to vocalize or identify. A preschooler is not going to say, "My mom is deployed, my dad is overwhelmed, and I am scared and feeling powerless and need reassurance and a sense of agency." Instead, that child may communicate this need by throwing tantrums or acting out against other children. Often challenging behaviors are simply children communicating about the classroom or the current state of their lives.

When we accept the theory that behavior is a form of communication, we must look at our role in dealing with children's behaviors differently. Traditionally, the focus has been on how a teacher *responds* to a behavior. Experts always seem to be offering new approaches to behavior modification. Time-outs, counting, positive reinforcement, behavior charts, and sending children to the office or home are all tools that teachers have used to attempt to influence children's behaviors—particularly those behaviors that are ongoing and especially challenging.

Generally, once a child exhibits a challenging behavior, a teacher reacts and hopes that the reaction will prevent the behavior from happening again. However, the behavior often recurs despite a teacher's attempts to change it. This is because teachers' reactions to behaviors do not get at the heart of the issue. In order to have a long-term impact on a behavior, an early educator must figure out what the child is communicating through that behavior. Once the teacher identifies and addresses the underlying issue, the child will no longer need to communicate it through challenging behavior. By proactively meeting the needs of children, we can reduce challenging behaviors in the early childhood classroom.

Fix the Environment, Not the Flower

My attendance at the CSEFEL and introduction to the Pyramid Model inspired me to reevaluate what it means to be an early educator. Up to that point, I had focused on "fixing" children, on finding ways to get them to conform to my expectations for their behavior in the classroom. Around the same time, I encountered the following quote from Alexander den Heijer, an inspirational speaker from the Netherlands: "When a flower doesn't bloom, you fix the environment in which it grows, not the flower." This provided me a new paradigm for understanding the role of a teacher—that of a gardener.

> By proactively meeting the needs of children, we can reduce challenging behaviors in the early childhood classroom.

The image of a gardener tending to a plant provides us with a different lens through which we can examine children's challenging behaviors. I am not a gardener, but I know many people, including my own children, who are. When faced with a plant that is not thriving, the dedicated gardener will, quite literally, leave no stone unturned in the quest to discover why: Does it need more (or less) water? Is it receiving enough sun? Is the soil providing the right nutrients? Does it require stakes or supports? All these factors may be affecting the plant's development. Rarely does a gardener throw up her hands and declare the plant unfit. Similarly, when a child exhibits challenging behaviors, what if instead of blaming the child, we first looked at the environment? What if we shifted our focus from "fixing" the child to adapting the conditions in which she spends many hours each day so that she can be successful?

About This Book

Too often when a young child is expelled from an early learning center, it is because a teacher or director decided that the child is "unfixable" and, therefore, cannot be successful in the classroom environment. Of course, educators are not all trying to be "fixers" of children. Many understand that behavior has complex underlying causes, but they still may struggle to find an effective approach. This book will challenge you to shift your mindset from that of an educator to that of a "teacher-gardener." When faced with challenging behaviors, the teacher-gardener accepts it as a challenge to adapt a growing child's environment and relationships so that the child can be successful and get to the business of learning, developing, and playing.

Chapter 1: Classroom Factors. The first task of a gardener is to make sure the soil is appropriate and prepared for a plant's success. In the same way, a teacher prepares for a child's success by building an appropriate and responsive classroom environment. This chapter provides you with many strategies to examine your classroom environment to ensure that it is appropriate for children's learning and development. I describe ten factors in early childhood classrooms that, depending on how they are addressed, can contribute to challenging behaviors. By addressing these factors, you can reduce the likelihood that children will act out in your classroom.

Chapter 2: Active Learning. Children are active learners. They learn best when their bodies and minds are actively engaged in the learning process. Building learning environments around the components of active learning is one of the most powerful proactive strategies you can use to reduce challenging behaviors. When you seek to teach in the ways children learn, as opposed to trying to get them to learn in the ways you want to teach, children are less likely to resort to challenging behaviors to communicate their frustration. This chapter defines what active learning looks like in practice and how you can create classroom spaces responsive to the learning needs of young children.

Chapter 3: Building Relationships with Children. Along with incorporating the tenets of active learning, the most important strategy you can use to avoid challenging behaviors is to build strong relationships with the children in your care. When you know and understand your children as individuals, you are better equipped to build a classroom that meets each child's unique needs. When children come into your classroom knowing that they are respected and appreciated, they are less likely to act out to get the attention they need and deserve. In this chapter, we will look at ways to develop these strong relationships with children.

Chapter 4: Teaching Social Skills. During their growth, plants may falter and need special attention to keep them on a path of optimal development. These supports, such as watering, staking, and weeding, are done in response to a plant's needs. They are not a gardener's attempts to punish a plant, but to support the plant's growth. In the same way, your targeted social and emotional supports in response to challenging behaviors serve to aid a child's growth. They are designed not to punish, but to teach alternative behaviors. Chapter 4 looks at some strategies teachers may use in response to problem behaviors. Some of these strategies are ineffective—they do not serve to teach children the skills they need to be successful in the classroom. Instead, they are focused on forcing children into compliance or punishing them for their lack of understanding of the rules or their inability to follow them. After examining those strategies that are ineffective, we will look at effective strategies for helping children learn and successfully meet classroom expectations. You can use these strategies to support children in getting along in the social environment of the early childhood classroom.

Chapter 5: The MoNSTeR Response to Challenging Behavior. Even as you shift your focus from punishment to support, you still need to respond to behaviors as they occur in the classroom. This chapter outlines a simple way for you to respond that keeps children safe, returns calm to everyone involved, and provides support and instruction for alternative behaviors.

Chapter 6: Unmet Social and Emotional Needs. At times, although well-supported, a plant may still struggle to grow. Instead of dismissing the plant as defective, the dedicated gardener strives to find ways for the plant to reach its potential. In the same way, even in the most responsive of classrooms, some children may express their need for special attention—perhaps due to circumstances at home or elsewhere in their lives—through their behaviors. In these instances, we must plan and deliver intensive interventions to help these children succeed. In chapter 6, we will look at ways you can address children's unmet social and emotional needs through the experiences you plan, the classroom you design, and your interactions with children.

Chapter 7: Family Partnerships. Early childhood communities are stronger when teachers and families work together for the benefit of children. This partnership is especially important when a child is struggling with challenging behaviors. When their child is wrestling to meet the behavioral expectations in the classroom, family members also struggle. At times, they feel powerless in the face of their child's perceived failure. They may feel like they are being blamed or, in turn, they may blame the teacher. When you build partnerships with families, you work together with them to better meet a child's needs. This chapter provides strategies for building family partnerships and conducting conferences as well as a five-step conflict resolution process to use with families.

Chapter 8: A Comprehensive Approach to Challenging Behaviors. Addressing challenging behaviors in the early childhood classroom is like peeling an onion. Each step reveals another layer of information that helps you design approaches that support a child's success. This chapter brings together all the strategies presented in the book into one comprehensive approach. You can follow a scenario step-by-step to see in action how the strategies laid out in this book are designed to prevent and address challenging behaviors.

Real-World Stories. Throughout the book, in light-brown boxes, are numerous anecdotes from early childhood classrooms I've worked in or observed over my career. Some of them are actual scenarios, reproduced exactly as they occurred, and some are compilations of various classroom situations. These stories illustrate the principles in the book, showing how they might play out in classrooms and helping teachers connect the theories with practice. Hopefully, these examples will help you see how you can use the ideas in this book to address real situations in your classroom.

Digital Content. Along with all the practical strategies presented in this book, you will benefit from additional digital resources designed to support your work in the classroom. These resources include customizable versions of the reproducible forms from the book that you can use to observe children and record their behavior, document family conferences, and detail plans to support children in the classroom. A PDF presentation summarizing the information presented in the book enables you to quickly refresh and communicate your knowledge of the main points as part of your professional development. See page 178 for instructions on how to download. Also available online is a PLC/Book Study Guide that helps communities of educators learn together how to design experiences and spaces in which all young children can develop and learn. Go to freespirit.com/PLC to download the guide.

How to Use This Book

This book is intended for all adults who are impacted by challenging behaviors in the early childhood classroom. While it is written for teachers, it will also be helpful for those who support teachers as program directors, managers, or providers of technical assistance. Parents of children who struggle with challenging behaviors may also benefit from the information provided in this book. The book is designed for professionals and families alike to take a critical look at the spaces and experiences we create for children and how those might be contributing to children's behaviors. It lays out a multistep process through which those who care for children can evaluate and adapt learning environments to better support children's needs. It will also guide adults in responding to problem behaviors in ways that are more likely to de-escalate situations and teach children the skills they need to be successful in meeting the social and emotional demands of the classroom.

> This book can help readers who are in the midst of dealing with challenging behaviors, but it can also be used proactively to help teachers create classroom environments in which challenging behaviors are less likely to occur.

This book can help readers who are in the midst of dealing with challenging behaviors, but it can also be used proactively to help teachers create classroom environments in which challenging behaviors are less likely to occur. Use this book to learn how to design spaces, plan routines and experiences, and interact with children so that they are more likely to be successful, thus eliminating their need for challenging behaviors. *Uncover the Roots of Challenging Behavior* is for all those who are dedicated to the optimal growth and development of young children—those who, like devoted gardeners, are committed to creating nurturing spaces in which all kids thrive.

◇◇

I spent seven years at that small early learning center in Detroit. My co-teachers and I spent hours attempting to translate and understand children's behaviors so we could adapt our practices to address their needs. We worked tirelessly to create a garden in which each "plant" was valued and tended to. Many days I went home exhausted and feeling helpless in the face of some especially perplexing behavior. But the victories were sweet and made the exhaustion worthwhile: seeing Kyra's mom in tears as her daughter graduated from preK after having been asked to leave seven other centers; overhearing Oscar proudly inform his grandmother that he had gone all day without hitting and had made a friend who wanted to play with him. Like the gardener who takes special pride in an abundant harvest, the teacher-gardener will take pride in a classroom community that benefits all children.

I'd love to hear how this book has helped you in your work with young learners. If you have stories to share or questions for me, you can reach me through my publisher at help4kids@freespirit.com or visit my website at michellesalcedo.com.

Michelle Salcedo, M.Ed.

Chapter 1

Classroom Factors:
Prepare the Soil for Growth

When teachers start to view themselves as gardeners, they begin to see that their role is not to fix children who present challenges, but instead to adapt classroom environments so that more children are likely to succeed. These approaches proactively address challenging behaviors, since sometimes these behaviors are communicating that classrooms are not appropriate for how children learn and develop. When teachers create environments shaped around children's needs, they can decrease incidents of challenging behaviors and increase learning.[5] These approaches benefit all children in the classroom and make it more likely that all children will thrive and less likely that challenging behaviors will occur.

Young children have not yet formed the ability to articulate, or even understand, the motivations behind their behaviors. When asked, "Why did you do that?" children may reply with a blank stare, an "I don't know," or a shrug of the shoulders. In most cases, these are not signs of defiance or apathy, but reflections of the truth.

A three-year-old will not walk into a classroom and say, "Listen, it was a rough night at home last night. Mom and Dad were arguing, and our family dinner turned into a shouting match. Nobody read me a story before bed, and this morning the tension was still so thick you could cut it with a knife. Mom stormed off to work without even giving me a kiss. So I'm probably going to need you to cut me some slack today." Instead, that child, when asked to stand in line, may dissolve into a tantrum or lash out angrily at the children near her. When asked why she behaved in such a way, she will not only be unable to articulate her motivations, but will not understand them or connect them to the situation that may be bothering her.

Young children usually do not know why they behave in certain ways, but their behaviors communicate to us that something is amiss. It is up to the teacher to translate children's behaviors to understand the reasons behind them. Often behaviors are telling us something about the classroom environment. For instance, the child in the previous example may need changes to her environment to help her feel calm and supported. Once the behavior is understood, teachers can adapt the environment so the child will be more likely to thrive.

In this chapter, we will examine ten factors in early childhood classrooms that, depending on how they are addressed, can contribute to challenging behaviors. These factors include aspects of the physical classroom environment as well as the social-emotional environment created by a teacher's response to students' needs. After introducing each factor, we will look at how it can impact children's behaviors and how teachers can transform it to help children be more successful. Adapting teaching practices and classroom spaces in response to children's communications creates the highly supportive environments and nurturing and responsive relationships highlighted in CSEFEL's pyramid (see figure 1 on page 3).

Factor 1: Appropriateness of Expectations

"To love someone is to strive to accept that person exactly the way he or she is, right here and now."—*Mister Rogers*

Many demands are put on children every day in the classroom. Some of these expectations are developmentally appropriate, and children can meet them without incident. Some of these expectations are inappropriate, and children may respond to them with challenging behaviors. The definition of an appropriate expectation is one that children are physically, emotionally, and cognitively ready to meet. When we focus on creating environments built around appropriate expectations, we benefit all children in the classroom.

The first step in addressing this factor is to examine each expectation by asking the following questions:

1. Is the expectation appropriate for children's level of development?

2. Is the expectation appropriate for a *particular* child in the current situation?

3. Is the expectation needed for children's safety or well-being?

Examples of Inappropriate Expectations in Early Childhood Classrooms

Following are some examples of common expectations that are often developmentally inappropriate in early childhood classrooms.

Circle Time

Ms. Kaitlyn facilitates a circle time that usually lasts fifteen minutes. After leading an active song, she asks the children to sit "crisscross applesauce" while she leads them in counting to ten in Spanish. Next, she lays out some pictures of fruits and vegetables for children to sort. She ends the group experience with another song before having children say which centers they are going to play in first.

Periodically, she has to deal with children who struggle with sitting still or who meddle with the children sitting around them. But generally, children sit passively during this part of the day. However, since four-year-old Brian joined her class, her circle times have not gone so well. She spends ten minutes convincing Brian to join the group. When he is on the carpet, he will not sit still. Instead, he would rather pull hair or kick others and seems to enjoy when they react strongly. When Ms. Kaitlyn tries to control or correct Brian, he runs around the classroom yelling and sometimes throwing toys. Circle time and the other children are forgotten as Ms. Kaitlyn has to deal with Brian. If she does manage to corral him, the other children have lost interest and she must spend extra effort to get them focused back on circle time.

Ms. Kaitlyn's focus in this situation is on "fixing" Brian so he sits during circle time and participates like the other children. She is focused on having him conform to her expectations of behavior. This is not wrong. She wants Brian to be able to function in a classroom setting, and she thinks that by placing these expectations on him she is helping him. However, what if instead of focusing on "fixing" Brian, Ms. Kaitlyn took on the role of a teacher-gardener and examined the classroom environment she has created to see how it might be contributing to his behavior? By shifting her expectations, she can create an environment in which Brian can be successful.

Let's look at Ms. Kaitlyn's situation through our three questions:

1. **Is the expectation appropriate for children's level of development?**
   We can say that typically, children in a prekindergarten classroom can sit and pay attention and can participate in a large group for a short period. So for most children, the expectation that children participate in a fifteen-minute circle time seems reasonable and appropriate.

2. **Is the expectation appropriate for a particular child in the current situation?**
   In this case, it is important to differentiate between the group and the individual. While it may be reasonable for a typical four-year-old to sit and participate in circle time, Brian is showing through his behavior that the expectation may not be appropriate for him, especially given that he is new to the classroom. Ms. Kaitlyn might consider that asking Brian to sit and participate in circle time may not be appropriate for him and that this expectation is the reason for his behavior.

3. **Is the expectation needed for children's safety or well-being?**
   Many times, teachers set expectations without really considering the reasons behind them. Why do we ask children to sit "crisscross applesauce"? Is it

unsafe for them to sit in another position? What if, instead, your rule for circle time was that children could participate however they were comfortable (in a chair, lying down, standing) as long as they didn't bother anyone else?

A bigger question may be if the expectation that children even *come* to circle time is one that is needed for their safety or well-being. While many teachers believe that children are better served if they participate in all aspects of classroom life, this expectation may not be appropriate for all children at all times.

In this instance, Brian is not benefiting from being required to participate in circle time. When Ms. Kaitlyn requires him to be there, he communicates that this expectation is not appropriate for him through his challenging behaviors. If Ms. Kaitlyn removes this expectation and lets him play in the classroom while she leads circle time, the behaviors may be avoided. Brian may follow along with circle time from another part of the room and eventually come to the gathering on his own when he is ready. Additionally, the other children would benefit from the circle time experience instead of having to wait while their teacher's attention is diverted by Brian's behavior.

When looked at through this lens, it becomes obvious that, in most cases, the expectation that all children always come to circle time and sit in a particular style does not benefit their safety or well-being. Hence, this requirement is inappropriate in the early childhood classroom. Upon this realization, some teachers express concern that if they remove this requirement, none of the children will want to participate in circle time activities. If this is the case, the bigger concern is that your circle time may not be engaging and interesting to children. We will talk more about that in chapter 2.

ASK "WHY NOT?"

On a tour of a center, I noticed a sign posted on three walls in the classroom that simply said, "Why not?" When I asked about the sign, the teacher explained her philosophy. Whenever she finds herself about to say "no" to a child or correct a behavior, she first pauses and asks herself, "Why not?" If the expectation she is about to impose on a child is not based on the child's safety or well-being, she instead engages with the child or stands back to observe the situation. She stated that since implementing this strategy, she has noticed that children are more engaged, challenging behaviors are down, and she has been surprised by what she has learned about the children.

What would change about your job if you replaced expectations for children's behavior with a "Why not?" philosophy?

Waiting

We know that children are not designed to wait. The typical child has an attention span of one to two minutes more or less than her age.[6] So, the typically developing three-year-old has an attention span of one to five minutes. When we put children in situations in which they must wait more than that, they may react with challenging behaviors.

Most teachers recognize that children are not designed to wait, and they create their daily routines to reduce waiting. Yet in many classrooms, waiting creeps unnoticed into the day. Some examples include:

Prepping for outside. The teacher must put sunscreen on each child before going outside. After choice time, she has children sit in a circle so she can make sure to get it on each one. By the time she has completed this task, children have been sitting and waiting for about thirty minutes.

Instead, in this situation, the teacher might put sunscreen on children during choice time. She could call children to her one by one to go through this routine. This way, all children are protected from the sun and no one has to wait. She can also take advantage of the one-on-one interaction to give individual attention to each child.

Running by the clock. Lunch is scheduled for noon. As children come in from outside at 11:30, the teacher has them wash their hands and sit at their tables so he can put out cots. Lunch is a couple of minutes late and arrives at 12:05. By the time the teacher serves the food, children have been waiting at the tables for more than twenty minutes.

A common tendency is to run the classroom by the clock instead of by what is happening in the life of the classroom that day. In this situation, children could be allowed to play until lunch is coming through the door. At this point, they could wash their hands and head to tables to eat.

Family-style meals in which children serve themselves make for even less waiting. The teacher sets the food in containers on the tables. Once children have washed their hands, they can set their places, sit down, serve themselves food, and begin to eat.

Waiting for pickup. As the end of the day nears, teachers begin to focus on making sure their rooms are ready for the following day. They may gather all children on a carpet and ask them to remain there with a book or a basket of manipulatives until they get picked up to go home. By the time the last child leaves, he has been sitting on the carpet for more than thirty minutes.

It is not an appropriate expectation that children prematurely disengage with the classroom to fit the needs of a teacher's schedule. Instead, it is a teacher's duty to interact with children as they explore the classroom until the end of the day. It is unrealistic to expect children to sit in one area with limited materials for a long time.

Waiting is one of those expectations that many teachers theoretically understand to be inappropriate for young children. Yet without realizing it, teachers often introduce waiting into the daily routine. When faced with challenging behaviors, teachers can take a step back and make sure an expectation around waiting is not the culprit.

Self-Control

Young children are learning how to make their way in the world. This includes learning how to control their bodies and impulses. At times, these impulses may contrast with the expectations teachers place on children.

Let's look at how these expectations for self-control may creep into classroom situations and impact children's behaviors.

> **Standing in line.** Before going outside, Ms. Ramona requires her toddlers to line up quietly. Naturally, as toddlers lack the ability to control their impulses, this time of day is challenging. By the time she gets the stragglers lined up, those who were already in line have become bored and have started to play, lie down, or leave the line altogether. Ms. Ramona becomes increasingly frustrated and says things like, "We will not go outside until everyone is ready." She wastes an inordinate amount of time trying to have children meet an expectation for self-control.

Instead, Ms. Ramona could have children gather at the door. Making sure they are all with her, she could move the group outside without requiring them to stand quietly in line before going through the door. By changing the expectation from "all children must stand quietly in line" to "I will get the class outside as quickly, safely, and efficiently as possible," the challenging behaviors that resulted from children not being able to meet this expectation disappear.

> **Sitting quiet and still.** Mr. Jacob values the importance of early literacy experiences, and he wants to make sure all children benefit from his daily storytimes. To make sure all children can see and are paying attention, the teacher has taped Xs on the carpet. He requires that all children sit on an X with their legs folded and their hands in their laps. Often, he must interrupt the story to reprimand children who are restless, wiggling around, and bothering others. These children indicate their inability to meet this expectation for self-control through their restlessness.

Child development expert Jean Piaget tells us that children are sensory-motor learners. They learn as they move and experience the world through their senses. We limit their ability to learn when we put expectations on them for bodily self-control. Expectations of self-control can be especially challenging for young boys. There is contradictory evidence on how testosterone might impact the ability of young boys to exhibit bodily control, yet surges of this hormone are thought to compel boys to action.[7] While a teacher is saying "crisscross applesauce" to a wiggling child, his body may be screaming, "I have to move!" In this situation, the bodily impulses will often win out, and the resulting movement may appear as a challenging behavior to a teacher.

As discussed previously, it is not necessary for children's safety or well-being that they sit in a particular way during group experiences. Teachers eliminate many challenging behaviors when they remove this expectation for self-control. Instead of sitting quiet and still, children can be expected to choose a position that enables them to pay attention to the teacher while not disturbing others. When children can sit comfortably, stand up, or pace, they are meeting their own developmental and learning needs. This will lead to gatherings that are much more meaningful and peaceful for everyone involved.

Teachers come into classrooms with many expectations for how children should behave. These expectations may be cultural, formed by a teacher's own experiences as a young person, and they often emerge from the best of intentions. Teachers want children to be successful in educational settings and in society. However, no matter the genesis of these expectations, they may be inappropriate for children's development. When a teacher is faced with challenging behaviors, it's essential that she examine her expectations to make sure that they are not at the root of the behaviors and, if necessary, reframe them to be more developmentally appropriate.

EACH STAGE OF CHILDHOOD IS COMPLETE IN ITSELF

At times, teachers put pressure on themselves to get children to behave in certain ways because "they are going to have to do it next year." This is the hallmark of a developmentally inappropriate expectation. We do not let teens who are too young to drive handle a car because "they are going to have to do it next year." Instead, we provide them with education and experiences so that when they are old enough to drive, they can do so successfully.

In the same way, we do not get a three-year-old ready to be four by treating her like she is already four. She will be a successful four-year-old when she is four. Now, it is her job to be three. Childhood is not a disease we need to cure as quickly as possible. Each stage of childhood should be valued and enjoyed.

The late, great Bev Bos had the following quote from J.C. Pearce hanging in her center: "Every stage of development is complete in itself. The three-year-old is not an incomplete five-year-old. The child is not an incomplete adult. Never are we simply on our way. Always we have arrived. Enjoy now."

Factor 2: Space Design

"Design is the application of intent—the opposite of happenstance, and an antidote to accident."—Robert L. Peters

The environments in which we find ourselves send messages to our brains about how we should behave. An important part of a classroom environment is how teachers use furniture and equipment to define spaces. The design of the classroom environment is so important in how it impacts children's behaviors and learning that it's referred to in Reggio Emilia as the "third teacher."[8] As Jim Greenman so eloquently says in his book *Caring Spaces, Learning Places: Children's Environments That Work*, "Space speaks to each of us. Long corridors whisper *run* to a child; picket fences invite us to trail our hands along the slats. Physical objects have emotional messages of warmth, pleasure, solemnity, fear; action messages of *come close*, *touch me*, *stay away*; or identity messages of *I'm strong*, or *I'm fragile* . . . Spaces do more than speak—they load our bodies and minds with sensory information."[9]

When teachers are faced with challenging behaviors, they need to look at the messages the space might be sending children, who spend forty to fifty hours a week in the classroom.

Examples of Problematic Space Design

Let's look at some common ways classroom design can contribute to challenging behaviors.

Static Classroom Arrangements

In Ms. Pam's classroom, the dramatic play area is extremely popular. Her classroom management system tells children that only three kids can be in the center at a time, but this always seems to cause problems. Sometimes children push others in their rush to be the first ones in their favorite center. Tantrums and arguments ensue when it is already full and children can't get in. At times children try to sneak in, only to be greeted by a chorus of "no" and "I'm telling" from those already in the center. Ms. Pam, frustrated by the behaviors she sees in this popular center, often ends up closing it in an attempt to teach children that their behavior is not appropriate.

After reading an article about the impact of classroom arrangement on children's behaviors, Ms. Pam decides to step back and observe how children are using the space. She also invites a coworker to observe and give her some ideas. After discussing their observations, the teachers notice that many of the challenging behaviors are due to the current popularity of the dramatic play area. After school, Ms. Pam and her director rearrange the space to make her dramatic play center bigger so it can accommodate more children. She then evaluates other centers to make sure that all of them have interesting materials for children to explore. She also incorporates more pretend play opportunities in the other centers so children find their interests reflected throughout the classroom. For example, she adds paper dolls and small furniture to the block center. She adds dishes and pretend food to the sensory table. She also makes sure that there are opportunities for pretend play when children are outside.

When the children return to the classroom the following day, they are excited to find their new space. They spread out around the room to investigate the new additions to the learning centers. Those still drawn to the dramatic play area find more space to move around, and more children can join in the play. By shifting her focus from punishing children for their behaviors to looking at what may be causing them, Ms. Pam discovers ways to set children up for success.

In the face of challenging behaviors, teachers need to take a step back and see how children are using centers and how the spaces might be contributing to these behaviors. In some instances, slight shifts in setup might extinguish problems by making the spaces more conducive to how children currently use them.

Cramped Learning Centers

Just like Ms. Pam, Ms. Kanessa struggles with challenging behaviors in one of her centers: the block center. Even when only two children are in the center, fights seem to break out in this area. Because of the narrow layout of the center, children often bump into each other's structures. They become frustrated and often lash out angrily when a structure comes toppling down. When children fight, Ms. Kanessa sends them into other centers or even closes the block center, but nothing she does seems to make a difference in children's behavior.

Once again, this center is not set up for children's success based on how they are using it. Young kids often struggle with impulse control. When someone bumps them or the structure they have so carefully constructed, they will often strike out in frustration. Because the block center is so narrow, those collisions are bound to happen. Ms. Kanessa can look at her classroom as a whole and find a way to restructure it so the block center allows more space for building.

Spaces That Encourage Running

"Walking feet" is rule number two on a posted list of rules in Ms. Gloria's preschool room. Despite this and constant reminders to use "walking feet," children run laps around tables that are lined up on one side of the classroom. Large undefined spaces scream "Run!" to a child who would like nothing more than an excuse to run, run, run through life. Running is not a challenging behavior in itself, but it can be dangerous in the classroom. In Ms. Gloria's classroom, accidents are common as children often bump into each other or collide with furniture as they run around.

If running often occurs in a classroom, the teacher's first step is to rearrange furniture and equipment so it cuts off the running paths. There are two classroom arrangements that can lead to running. The first is a large open area set aside for circle and group times. The other is an arrangement in which tables are lined up cafeteria-style on one side of the classroom. Both setups provide running tracks for children and can lead to overcrowding in other centers as they are squeezed into the remaining space.

Open Learning Centers

Learning centers with open boundaries often create pathways that cause children to disrupt each other's play, which may lead to confusion and fighting. Here's an example:

> Four children are working hard in the dramatic play center to set up a picnic for themselves and their babies. Because the center is in front of the bathrooms and sinks, other children cross over the picnic blanket, scattering the dishes and interrupting the picnic play. Cries of frustration turn into cries of pain as one of the picnickers pushes another child into a shelf because he kicked over her baby on his way back from the bathroom.

With this classroom design, conflicts should be expected. Some centers, such as the block and pretend play centers, are more conducive to social and constructive play that, unfortunately, can easily be interrupted. Challenging behaviors will decrease when classrooms are arranged so that centers are large enough for this type of play and situated where other children do not have to pass through them to get to other parts of the classroom.

Furniture Placement

> Ms. Keisha is frustrated because her toddlers seem to be more interested in dumping all the toys from the shelves instead of playing with them. She spends her time scooping manipulatives back into baskets instead of interacting with children. By the end of free choice time, the classroom is in chaos. All the toys are on the floor, and children are throwing them or running around uninterested in the materials in the classroom.

In her classroom, Ms. Keisha has arranged the furniture so that all the shelves are on the carpet, facing each other in a large square and two tables are placed on the tiled section of the room. Upon closer examination, it is easy to see how this arrangement contributes to how children are using the materials. The shelves form a rectangular play space on the carpet. As children remove the toys, they are crowded together and have no guidance as to how they are expected to use the materials. In the absence of these physical clues, children either quickly drop their selected toy to find something else or play with the toy in an inappropriate manner. And as children are limited to the small space on the carpet, they often bump into each other and interfere with each other's play. With some simple furniture rearrangement, Ms. Keisha can define learning centers for children, spread them throughout the classroom to lessen physical confrontations, and help children understand the expectations for using the materials.

Teachers can use their furniture arrangements to help children understand how to use learning centers. It is tempting to place tables close together on tiled areas so that it's easier to supervise and assist children as well as clean up after them. But when tables are arranged in this way, children are less likely to use them during play since they are not placed next to a shelf with accessible materials. Likewise, when shelves are all grouped together, often on the carpet, children may not understand how various toys can be used differently—for example, some used on the floor, some used on tables, and some used while standing. Also, shelves placed close together in one section of the room force children to play in close proximity to one another. With this arrangement, children watch how others are using the materials and may copy behaviors that look like more fun, such as throwing or dumping toys.

Instead of automatically thinking "tile beneath tables for eating" and "carpet beneath shelves in centers," teachers can look at their classroom as a blank canvas. Tables and shelves can be placed where they make sense, not how the flooring suggests. An arrangement in which tables and shelves are paired with purpose throughout the classroom can help children understand how to use materials.

For example, a manipulatives shelf placed next to a table sends the message that children can use the materials from the shelf on the table, instead of throwing them in the air or dumping them on the ground. Likewise, a block shelf placed on carpet and facing a wall indicates to children that they can build with the blocks on the floor. Also, spreading out the shelves and facing them in different directions helps children understand that different play happens in the separate areas created by the furniture arrangement. Additionally, this disperses children across the classroom so they are not playing so close together.

In Ms. Keisha's classroom, rearranging the furniture to create clear shelf-and-table centers reduces the challenging behaviors that leave her frustrated. For example, she moves one of the shelves next to a table on the tiles. On this shelf, she places art materials that she wants children to use on the table. Next, she moves one of the tables next to a shelf on the carpet and places puzzles and other manipulatives on this shelf so children use them on the table instead of the floor. She turns the other shelves so they are facing in opposite directions and defines a block center and a pretend play center. By spreading out and defining the centers, Ms. Keisha helps her children understand how to use the materials, thus eliminating the challenging behaviors that resulted from this factor.

In all the examples in this section, the challenging behaviors could have been avoided through intentional and appropriate classroom arrangement. Teachers can use furniture, floor coverings, and learning center arrangements to communicate behavioral expectations and help children meet these expectations in the classroom.

Factor 3: Material Options

"Sometimes the best learning environment for students isn't a bunch of devices powered by Wi-Fi. Sometimes it's a huge pile of cardboard powered by pure imagination."—Krissy Venosdale

Many children spend upwards of forty-five hours in a classroom each week. With this much time in a space, it is important that teachers pay attention to what they provide to occupy children's time and interests. If children aren't engaged by classroom materials, they will seek out mental and physical engagement elsewhere. The ways they find to amuse themselves may appear as challenging behaviors, although in reality, children are just communicating that the materials in their classroom are not appropriate in some way.

Types of Problems with Materials

The messages about classroom materials that children are sending through their behaviors can typically be grouped into three categories: the materials are too few, too many, or developmentally inappropriate.

Too Few Materials

When classroom shelves are empty, children will look for ways to keep their brains and bodies occupied, which may be perceived by teachers as challenging behaviors.

When you look around Ms. Symone's two-year-old classroom, the lack of materials is evident. Most of her shelves have only two or three toys, puzzles are missing pieces, books are ripped and incomplete, and the dramatic play area is just a simple plastic kitchen set and a couple of naked baby dolls.

Not surprisingly, challenging behaviors are frequent in this classroom. Children bite as they fight over materials. During free playtime, children climb on and jump off the tables and shelves. They often fall and hurt themselves as they run around and trip or crowd each other. No matter how Ms. Symone reacts to these behaviors, children continue to act disruptively in the classroom.

In this instance, children will continue to exhibit these behaviors as long as activities for them in the classroom are insufficient. While it may not always be possible to buy lots of new materials for a classroom, teachers can make or find many items to enhance children's play environments (see **figure 1.1** for ideas). Children are less likely to resort to challenging behaviors for entertainment when classrooms are places of wonder filled with interesting materials to explore.

Figure 1.1 Teacher-Made and Found Classroom Materials

Sensory bottles: Add any combination of liquid and solids to clear, clean plastic bottles. For example, you might fill a bottle with clear hair gel and add beads. Or, fill the bottle with a mixture of water and oil and add paper clips. Securely seal the bottles by hot-gluing the tops closed before giving them to children to explore.

Musical bottles: Add any material that makes noise to clean plastic bottles. Securely seal the bottles before giving them to children.

Building materials: Bring in cardboard boxes and tubes, egg cartons, plastic cups, and wine shipping containers. (Note: Because of their unique shape, wine bottles are shipped in interesting cardboard cartons. Those cartons can add variety to children's construction or art projects. Ask your local wine shop for empty cartons.)

Daily life materials: Ask families to send in their old clothes, cell phones (with SIM cards and batteries removed), old plastic dishes, clean empty food boxes and spice jars, and other kitchen materials for pretend play.

Fabric strips: Cut up old towels and sheets into pieces. Children can use them for dancing, dress-up, and art.

Magazines, newspapers, catalogs, and ads: Pictures from these can be used for art, memory games, and sorting activities.

Homemade puzzles: Attach pictures to pieces of cardboard. Cut these into pieces to make puzzles.

Homemade playdough: Make playdough using the following recipe. Add different colors, spices, and textures (rice, oats, grass) to the dough to vary the sensory experience for children.

- Mix 2 cups flour, ½ cup salt, 2 tablespoons cream of tartar, and 2 tablespoons oil in a large mixing bowl.
- Add food coloring (optional) to 1½ cups hot water. Add the water to the dry ingredients.
- Stir continuously until it becomes a sticky, combined dough.
- Allow the dough to cool, then take it out of the bowl and knead it vigorously for a couple of minutes until all the stickiness is gone. If it remains a little sticky, add a touch more flour until it is just right. (Note: If the playdough is too sticky, it will be messier and not as much fun.)

Water play: Children love playing in water (as evidenced by their fascination with toilets!). If you do not have a sensory table, you can fill bins or large bowls with water. Add soil, soap, ice, toys, measuring cups and spoons, and the like to provide different experiences.

Shoes: Ask families to send in old shoes. Children can use them to sort, make patterns, paint, play dress-up, and stack, among other things.

Jar and bottle caps: Add a collection of jar and bottle caps to your math center. Children will use them to sort, make patterns, seriate, and make lines and shapes. Add index cards with shapes and letters to extend the play.

Too Many Materials

On the flip side, challenging behaviors can also be the result of classrooms stuffed with too many materials. Children can become overwhelmed when there are too many choices. They are more likely to be engaged and use materials appropriately when they can see their choices clearly.

A formula teachers can use to make sure their learning centers are neither over nor understocked is that a learning center should have three choices for each child who can be in the center at a time. So, if four children can be in the math and manipulatives center, there should be twelve choices for activities. This formula ensures that each child can find something to do and is not overwhelmed by the sheer number of choices. Instead of having everything always out and available, the teacher can rotate materials so children are continuously surprised by what they find in the classroom.

Developmentally Inappropriate Materials

Along with the number of materials, the developmental level of the materials is also important. Challenging behaviors can be a result of developmentally inappropriate material choices in the classroom. When children are neither sufficiently engaged, challenged, nor entertained, they may express that through their behaviors.

MATERIALS ARE TOO EASY OR LACK INTEREST

Toward the end of the day at an early learning center, the three-year-old children left in Ms. Tatiana's classroom are moved into Ms. Terry's two-year-old classroom so Ms. Tatiana can go home. Ms. Terry dreads this time of the day because two of the children who come into her classroom are often difficult for her to manage. Instead of playing with the toys as the other children do, they prefer to throw the toys or dump them all on the floor and kick them around. Unfortunately, the other children see this and lose interest in their activities, instead emulating the disruptive behaviors. Upon investigation, Ms. Terry finds that these two children only exhibit these behaviors in her classroom. They are engaged and properly use materials when they are in their own classroom. Out of frustration, she often resorts to sending the two children to the director's office. Despite this and many conversations with the children's families, the behaviors persist.

Ms. Terry's attempts to change the children's behaviors will not be successful until she figures out what the behaviors are communicating and fixes the factors causing the behaviors. In this case, the older children are not interested in or challenged by the materials in the two-year-old classroom. They are bored with the material choices, so they find different ways to entertain themselves. Upon realizing that the lack of age-appropriate materials is causing the challenging behaviors, the director and Ms. Terry look for solutions. They create boxes of materials that will be more engaging for the older children, yet are still safe for the younger group to use. For example, one box may contain a special smelly version of playdough and many interesting tools for exploring it. Another box might have interesting and open-ended manipulatives that only come out at the end of the day. When the three-year-olds are blended into the younger classroom, Ms. Terry brings out these materials. She also has conversations with Ms. Tatiana to understand more about the two children who have been engaging in challenging behavior. Once she understands their interests, she plans specific materials and activities to appeal to them.

Challenging behaviors in response to a lack of interesting materials are especially common in classrooms hosting school-age kids (ages six and up) for after-school care. Often, centers place children in this age group in rooms that are used, most of the day, for younger children. Or, classrooms are pieced together from furniture and materials harvested from other rooms. School-age children have a lot of energy after being in school all day and are looking for ways to release that energy, have some fun, and engage in interesting activities. When these opportunities aren't present, they often react with challenging behaviors, which may include swearing, defiance, and picking on others. When teachers provide environments that are specially designed to engage school-age children physically and mentally, these behaviors are less likely to occur. See **figure 1.2** for ideas.

Figure 1.2 Incorporating School-Age Materials into Early Childhood Classrooms

Note: When incorporating materials for school-age children into young children's classrooms, make sure that all materials are safe for all children or that the younger children cannot access inappropriate materials.

INTEREST CENTER	ENHANCEMENT IDEAS
Blocks	• Boxes • Recycled materials (egg cartons; fabric pieces; cardboard tubes, boxes, and sheets) • Fabric • Stones • Pieces of wood • Pictures of interesting buildings to inspire children's structures
Dramatic play	• Allow children to decide how to set up the area for pretend play and let them find the materials they need. • Children can decorate large pieces of cardboard (unfolded boxes) to make backdrops for scenarios. • Set up a stage and let children put on performances. • Designate an area as a photo booth. Children can set up various backdrops and gather props. They can either pretend to take pictures or draw pictures of each other, or staff can take actual pictures of them in the photo booth.
Games	• Use wall space to create large vertical versions of children's favorite games, for example, Tetris and Connect Four. • Bring in special visitors to teach children games like chess, checkers, mancala, cribbage, and so on. • Host tournaments of popular games.
Science	• Invite families to send in old appliances like vacuums. Cut off the cords and challenge children to take apart the machines and reassemble them. • Include natural items, such as leaves and rocks from children's neighborhoods, for great additions to this center. • Provide some appliance owner's manuals to give children a peek into the inner workings of the complex machines they might see in their homes. • Build a "potion station" and provide containers and safe liquids (baby oil, baby shampoo) and solids (soil, flour, cornstarch) for children to mix.
Art	• School-age children can make amazing pieces of art with almost anything. Make sure you have the basics (paint, paper, glue) available. • Add recycled materials, such as cardboard, fabric pieces, magazines, corks, wire, tops and lids, yarn or string, old jewelry, and so on.
Writing	• Post interesting story prompts to inspire children's creative writing. For example, "I was surprised to wake up to find my arms were replaced with wings." • Post weekly riddles to challenge children's thinking.

Figure 1.2 Incorporating School-Age Materials into Early Childhood Classrooms (continued)

Writing (continued)	• Ask children about people they admire. Find addresses for those people and encourage children to write letters to them. • Under your supervision, challenge children to research a historical figure and create a social media account (Facebook, Twitter) for him or her. • Engage children in building a word wall. Pick a child every day to look through the dictionary and find an interesting word to add to the wall. Can the other children guess what it means? • Challenge children with word games. Write the word *big* on a large piece of paper. Invite children to write different words they could use instead of *big*. How many words can they add to the list? • Have word searches, crosswords, and other word games available.

Movement	• School-age children need opportunities to move and exert energy after spending all day in school. You can creatively add in materials that allow them to safely use their large muscles in the classroom:
	  » Rolled-up socks and boxes provide opportunities to throw.
	  » Beach balls hanging from the ceiling allow children to jump and hit.
	  » Two-liter plastic bottles filled with marbles, nuts and bolts, or rice provide weights for lifting or shaking.
	  » Rolled-up newspapers provide ripping challenges.
	  » Noisemaking items mounted slightly out of children's reach on a wall can provide them with safe jumping goals.
	  » A posted picture of a treadmill control panel, a rectangle made from black tape on the floor, and a timer can create the illusion of a treadmill and a safe place to run in place.

Clubs	• Implement a club program in your school-age classroom. Clubs allow children to meet with others who share their interests and to explore new topics. • Children can sign up to be part of a club that meets once or twice during the week. • The club can be guided by the children themselves. Or, an adult may want to share a hobby with children for a designated period (for example, three months). • Some ideas for clubs may be a sport, a foreign language, knitting, chess, art, exercise, babysitting, and so on. • Rotate club offerings so children can explore many different topics.
General classroom	• School-age children do not want to spend their time in a "baby space." Ask for their help in designing their classroom. What posters or pictures can they bring from home to decorate the space? • Have a "design our room" challenge and give small groups of children a section of the classroom to design.

REPETITIVE MATERIALS

Seeing the same materials in the classroom day in and day out can cause a similar lack of interest in children. Teachers can rotate materials so children will often find something new as they explore the interest centers. To maintain children's interest and pique their intellectual curiosity, the Reggio Emilia approach challenges teachers to use *provocations*. Provocations are open-ended materials integrated into the classroom that reflect children's current interests or extend a project or thought. For example, in spring when children are observing the world in bloom, placing interesting flowers or plants in the art center may inspire their drawing and painting. If children have been to the beach, a teacher might add sand and shells to a sensory table to engage them and extend their thinking. These materials might provoke an idea or spur a question that leads to investigation. When teachers provide provocations that reflect children's interests and rotate materials often, there is no need for children to use challenging behaviors to communicate their boredom with a stale or unengaging classroom environment.

MATERIALS ARE TOO CHALLENGING

At times, children's behaviors may be communicating not that materials are too easy or lack interest, but that they are too challenging for children's developmental level. Psychologist Lev Vygotsky talks of children's *zone of proximal development*, that sweet spot where children can engage in activities on their own without adult support. This zone bridges what children can do by themselves and what they are unable to do. Sometimes teachers think that providing children with challenging materials will lead to increased learning. However, if children cannot engage with the materials on their own, not only will they not learn, but they will become increasingly frustrated. This frustration will often be displayed in tantrums or misuse of the materials. Thus, teachers need to know the developmental levels of the children in their classrooms and provide both materials they can use without adult help as well as some they can use with support. As any group of children will have varying levels of development, materials that will meet different children where they are must be available. Open-ended materials that can be used in a variety of ways are most likely to meet the diverse learning needs and interests of all children in the classroom.

When children spend most of their waking hours in a classroom, it is up to their teachers to provide a wide enough variety of materials to engage and challenge them. Sometimes challenging behaviors may be communicating that there are too few or too many materials or that the materials are not appropriate for the children in the class. When teachers provide just the right amount of materials that stimulate and engage children's brains and bodies, children will no longer need to engage in challenging behaviors to communicate about this factor.

Factor 4: Teacher Responsiveness

"An ideal culture is one in which there is a place for every human gift."
—Margaret Mead

Children are naturally egocentric. *Egocentrism* is defined as having little to no regard for interests, beliefs, or attitudes other than one's own; self-centered. With young children, egocentrism is to be expected. It is due to their brains not being fully developed and their lack of social experience and understanding. When classroom teachers are not responsive to children's needs and interests, children may communicate their lack of engagement through their behaviors. This lack of responsiveness in the classroom can be seen in two ways: how teachers plan their lessons and how they incorporate students' interests in the classroom.

Lesson Planning: Themes vs. Projects

Themes have been common in the preschool world for many years. When asked why they use themes in lesson planning, teachers often say they haven't given it much thought. Themes are so pervasive in early childhood classrooms that many teachers might think they are a required component of a curriculum. Teachers can use themes to organize their ideas: Themes help teachers know when to sing the songs, facilitate the art projects, read the stories, and plan the small-group experiences that are related to the current theme. A theme-driven curriculum also serves to assure families that teachers are addressing a variety of topics over the course of a year.

However, themes, while useful to a teacher, have very little benefit for children since they are not necessarily responsive to children's interests. For example, if a child is interested in the worms that surface after a rainstorm, more learning will happen if a teacher delves into the world of worms rather than spending energy trying to get the child engaged in the current theme of community helpers.

The Project Approach

One alternative to a theme-based curriculum is the project approach. This approach, detailed in the wonderful book *Engaging Children's Minds: The Project Approach* by Lilian Katz, Sylvia Chard, and Yvonne Kogan, builds in-depth investigations from children's interests, questions, and curiosities. Instead of basing curriculum on external elements, such as the calendar or what adults think children should be studying, teachers plan lessons based on what they notice about children's interests.

The project approach is an intricate dance between teacher and student. The teacher notices what engages children and plans classroom experiences and material enhancements for them to investigate their interests. During these activities, teachers interact with children and have conversations with and observe them to understand their thinking and the questions they have. These new understandings are then used to plan activities to further the investigations. The duration of the project is determined by children's engagement, lasting only as long as children are interested and learning and spinning in different directions based on children's curiosities.

This approach assumes that children are capable learners and honors the knowledge and experience they bring to the classroom. Instead of following a predetermined course of study that focuses on covering as many topics as possible, the project approach uncovers layer after layer of a topic that is interesting to children. By observing children and planning curriculum based on those observations, a teacher creates a classroom that is responsive to children's learning needs. Let's look at an example of the project approach in action.

During the first weeks of school, Ms. Lizzy plans open-ended experiences that allow her to get to know children and that allow children to get to know each other and the classroom. She takes advantage of this period to observe children and figure out what experiences and material enhancements she might use to engage them. She notices that many of the children are fascinated with the sinks and toilets in the classroom and that the water table is popular, so she decides to build a study around water. She starts the study with a KWL chart to find out what children already *know* about water, what they *want* to know about it, and what they *learn* through the study. She uses this information to plan learning experiences that build on children's knowledge and address some of their questions.

At first, the study focuses on exploring water and its properties. As she interacts with children, Ms. Lizzy hears many of them talk about how water is used in their homes, so she takes the study in that direction. Children spend the next couple of weeks washing play clothes and baby dolls, cleaning parts of the classroom, planting and caring for plant seeds, and following simple recipes that have water as an ingredient. During this time, Ms. Lizzy notices that many children show great interest in different aspects of the clothing they washed, so she begins to incorporate new experiences that delve into the world of clothing and uniforms.

This cycle of observing children, planning experiences, interacting with children, and planning new experiences based on new knowledge is the basis of Ms. Lizzy's curriculum decisions. Each year is different, as it unfolds based on the unique needs and interests of each group of children.

Another important difference between the project approach and classroom themes is how widely the topic of study permeates the learning. With themes, teachers tend to reflect the theme in all aspects of the curriculum: songs, fingerplays, artwork, stories, small-group activities, and games. With the project approach, teachers reflect children's interests in certain aspects of the curriculum, but they don't feel the need to tie *every* experience to a particular course of study. Let's revisit Ms. Lizzy's classroom for an example of this.

While Ms. Lizzy incorporates children's interest in water and clothing into some of the activities and material enhancements, she also continues to plan regular open-ended experiences to engage children. For example, she places step stools and boxes in the block center, not because they are related to the water study, but because she wants to challenge children to build on different levels. Along with planning some experiences to further children's interest and understanding of the current topic, she also plans some experiences because they support children's general learning, because they reflect the interests of individual children, or just because they are fun and appropriate for children.

RESOURCES FOR THE PROJECT APPROACH

You can learn much more about the project approach and how to implement it in your classroom through any of the following resources:

- The Project Approach website: projectapproach.org

- *Engaging Children's Minds: The Project Approach* by Lilian G. Katz, Sylvia C. Chard, and Yvonne Kogan

- "The Project Approach to Teaching and Learning" by Sylvia C. Chard (communityplaythings.com)

Reflecting Students' Interests in the Classroom Environment

Of course, it is highly unlikely that all children will be interested in the same topic at the same time. When planning curriculum, teachers can create a responsive classroom by intentionally considering the varied interests of the children in the group. Teachers can create an atmosphere of caring and inclusiveness by reflecting children's diverse interests in how they enhance the classroom. Some children may be enthralled with the latest princess movie, so add a castle cutout to the block center. If a child is in love with horses, nothing says "I notice you and care about you" like adding a book about horses to the library or singing a horse song at circle time. A dynamic classroom changes to reflect the revolving interests of the children within.

As teachers, we can spend a lot of time and energy trying to get children interested in what we want to teach. Or, we can figure out what they are interested in and dive into the learning with them. When teachers are responsive and classrooms are dynamic, children are more engaged in the learning. A child who feels like a valued part of the classroom community is less likely to feel disenfranchised and is, therefore, less likely to resort to challenging behaviors.

Factor 5: Sensory Stimulation

"I love church buildings, particularly cathedrals, and I like living in spaces that remind me of music or evoke that creative energy."—*Laura Mvula*

Join me for a minute for a quick trip. Travel with me through Times Square, the New York City destination emblematic of New Year's Eve revelry and raucous celebration. Even if you have not been there in person, you probably have seen it on TV as the ball drops to kick off a new year. Imagine you are standing in the middle of the square. What do you notice? You might describe the scene with words like *colorful, bright, busy, crowded, tall, cold* (as in lack of nature as opposed to temperature), and *noisy*.

Now, picture in your head the typical early childhood classroom. How many of the words used to describe Times Square are also applicable to the classroom?

Colorful. So many classrooms are filled with primary colors. From the furniture to the carpets to the materials that fill the shelves, we seem to have decided that a child's world should be awash in color.

Bright. In many of our classrooms, bright fluorescent lights glare overhead. In some states and provinces, those lights are required to be on all day, even during naptime.

Busy. In Times Square, flashing billboards and entrancing displays fight for your attention. It is hard to know where to focus; there is so much to take in. That same busyness can be found in many classrooms. Walls, backs of doors, and shelves are covered with charts, posters, labels, student artwork, and teacher-made displays. With so much to see, children often do not know what truly merits their attention.

Crowded. It may not feel like the classroom is crowded if you are an adult standing above children. But for a child who must share space, materials, and attention with many others of the same size, it may often feel like you are in the middle of a dense crowd.

Tall. In Times Square, imposing skyscrapers tower overhead. In early childhood classrooms, the walls, windows, displays, and shelves reach high above young children's heads. This adds to their sense of smallness in a big adult world.

Cold. The buildings of Times Square are constructed of metal, glass, and concrete. Neon lights, asphalt streets, and cement sidewalks add to the mechanical and cold environment. Any sense of nature is overpowered by the coldness of the facades. In some early childhood classrooms, plastic and shiny surfaces contribute to a nature-deprived environment. Nature, if there is any at all, might simply be a plant on top of a shelf or a small pet tucked away in a cage in a corner. Richard Louv, author of *Last Child in the Woods*, discusses in depth the price we pay as a society for raising children in a world in which they will best remember the smell and feel of plastic.

Noisy. In many classrooms, noise is a constant. Children's voices rise to compete with background noises like music or the sounds of battery-fueled toys. Early childhood environments, like Times Square, are filled with sounds that range from excited to frantic.

There are many ways an early childhood classroom might resemble Times Square. If you have ever been to Times Square, or to any large, crowded urban area, you know the energy is palpable. Upon entering the environment, a person's brain is flooded with messages. These messages cause the body to react in a variety of ways—from shutting down and fleeing the environment to excitedly diving in and embracing the chaos. Whether or not the energy of Times Square is attractive to you, there is no doubt that the sensory overload causes people to behave in ways they wouldn't in other environments. It is a place, for example, where a woman in a sweatshirt that reads "Minnesota's Nicest Grandmother" may channel her inner pro wrestler and push other tourists out of her way to get to a cart of cheap sunglasses and purses. While this is not how she would behave at home, the sensory overload to her brain causes an increase of adrenaline, and her behavior reflects this altered state of mind.

In the same way, children's challenging behaviors can be communicating that they are experiencing sensory overload in a classroom. If we are asking children to spend eight to ten hours a day, four to five days a week, in Times Square, we should not be surprised when they shut down or strike out in response to the environmental stimuli flooding their brains. When teachers create a learning space that provides less chaotic sensory input to the brain, challenging behaviors decrease.

Reducing Sensory Overload

Let's look at how to minimize the impact of each of the Times Square classroom components we've just discussed.

Neutralize Color

A good first step in moving away from a Times Square atmosphere is to reduce the color saturation of a classroom. For a time, early educators, designers, and families alike thought that everything for children had to be bright and colorful. Now we know that overusing bright colors can rile up children and cause excitement. Too much color can create an overstimulating atmosphere that can contribute to challenging behaviors, especially when children spend hours at a time surrounded by such color saturation.

Look instead to a more neutral palette for walls, furniture, and carpets. Soft, warm colors can create a calmer and more welcoming environment. There will still be plenty of color in the classroom materials and in children's artwork and clothing.

LIGHTEN IT UP

On a visit to Texas, I had a conversation with an early learning center director from the area. She told me that she had recently painted one of her classrooms. The room had been a bright blue, and she had covered that with a soft cream color. Her objective was to cover peeling paint and improve the look of the classroom, but she reported a wonderful, unexpected outcome of her decision. She observed that children's behaviors in the classroom changed. The children seemed calmer and more focused, and the general feeling of the classroom was more controlled and less hectic. As nothing else had changed except the color of the walls, she attributed this dramatic change to her decision to neutralize the wall color.

Many times, teachers have no control over the color of the walls or equipment in the classroom. So focus on what you *can* control. For example, you might hang neutral-colored fabrics on brightly colored walls. Instead of bright butcher paper and borders, use natural fabrics and neutral borders on bulletin boards and to frame children's artwork. Replace colorful bins with clear tubs, natural-fiber baskets, and even cardboard boxes that children can label and decorate.

Reduce Brightness

Many classrooms feature overhead fluorescent lights. The constant yellow glare of these bulbs can wear on children and adults alike. If possible, turn off some of the overhead lights in your classroom. Create gentle pools of light with lamps and natural light, as allowed by your local regulations. These forms of light are less glaring and can create different moods in different areas of the classroom, which can help children understand how to behave in those places. For example, a softly lit lamp in a cozy area can send the message that this is a place to relax. A floor lamp in the pretend play center creates a more homelike atmosphere that might inspire children's play. Directed spotlights in a science center can highlight different materials and provoke a sense of wonder and investigatory spirit in a child. As you go through your daily life, notice how businesses and other places use lighting to create moods and suggest behaviors, and draw inspiration for how you can use these ideas in your classroom.

If you are required to keep the overhead lights on, you can find many commercial products that replace traditional fluorescent light covers with nature scenes or covers that block some of the glare emitted by the lights. Alternatively, you can soften overhead lights by draping fabric just under them to diffuse the light. Or, adhere clear sticky paper on the outside of the coverings to reduce the brightness. Fire marshals have differing regulations regarding lighting, so make sure whatever solution you select is in line with your local regulations.

Reduce Visual Busyness

You can also make your classroom a calmer environment by decreasing the visual "noise" covering the walls and other flat surfaces. Many times, teachers believe that classroom displays expose children to important ideas and help them learn. In reality, many children do not often interact with a standard alphabet chart or a poster of classroom rules. This may be because there is so much on the walls that children don't know where to look. It may also be because many of the displays and posters are not terribly relevant to children. Whatever the reason, if posted materials are not of interest or use to children, they do not need to be there.

Teachers can reduce visual busyness by being more intentional in what they put on the classroom walls. Regularly evaluate your wall displays to make sure they relate to your current study and are useful, relevant, and meaningful to children. *Useful* displays are those that children interact with on a regular basis. *Relevant* displays are those that add information to a topic children are currently studying. *Meaningful* displays are those that somehow connect personally to children and their interests. Teachers often create displays that they hope will support children's learning, but unless the displays are useful, relevant, and meaningful, these tools often just become part of the visual noise of the classroom. In this case, you have two choices: remove the display or work to integrate it into classroom life.

EVALUATE AND ADAPT CLASSROOM DISPLAYS

Let's look at how teachers can adapt some common classroom displays to be useful, relevant, and meaningful and to prevent them from being empty visual noise.

Alphabet, number, color, and shape charts. Typically, these charts feature cartoon pictures that correspond to the letters of the alphabet, numbers, colors, or shapes. Often the images on the charts are not ones children necessarily know or care about. Also, the charts are usually posted high on the wall, out of children's direct view.

The first step in evaluating a display is to determine if it is relevant to children. An alphabet chart in an infant room, for example, is not developmentally appropriate and should be removed to reduce the visual stimulation in the room. Likewise, most four-year-olds already know color names, so a color chart is no longer needed. And if there is a child in the room who is not yet familiar with the color names, a poster placed high on the wall showing random colored objects is not going to teach them to him. It is not useful or meaningful. This can be removed to reduce busyness.

The truth is that children don't learn basic concepts from classroom displays. These ideas are learned through interactions between children and teachers using real materials. However, you can make wall charts more useful, relevant, and meaningful so they support learning goals.

◆ First, a chart becomes more *useful* when it is hung at children's eye level and placed where they can see and interact with it. For example, an alphabet chart is more likely to be used when it is placed in a writing area. A number line becomes more useful when it is near a math center. Another option is to turn posters into books or games. Cut them up and make a letter, number, color, or shape book for your library or other area in the classroom. Children are more likely to use and learn from materials if they can hold them, play matching games with them, and peruse them individually or in small groups, ideally with teacher interaction.

◆ Second, a chart becomes more *relevant* when it relates to something children are interested in or currently studying. Often, charts are hung on a wall and left there all year. Charts take on relevance when they are rotated and when they are referred to by teachers and children. For example, as a class is immersed in a study about water, a teacher might bring out a chart that shows the water cycle and use it as a basis for a small-group study with children. After the small group, the teacher hangs the chart in the science area, along with materials that children can use for hands-on exploration of water. As the teacher interacts with children in this area, she draws their attention to the chart and points out information that is relevant to their current investigations. As children move on to other aspects of a study, the teacher removes the chart and puts it away for another time when it may once again be relevant.

◆ Finally, a chart becomes more *meaningful* when children have a role in creating it. For alphabet charts, consider inviting children to find items that start with each letter of the alphabet. Take pictures of children with these items, and use these pictures to make an alphabet chart that adds more than just visual noise to the classroom. Do the same with number and color charts by having children gather items that represent numbers or colors. One classroom teacher made a color chart by putting together pictures of children holding out their hands dipped in paints of various colors. These charts have the bonus of reflecting the diversity of the children and families in the learning community.

Word walls. Word walls can play an important role in preK and kindergarten classrooms. As with all other classroom displays, if word walls are useful, relevant, and meaningful, they can help children develop interest in words. When children begin to connect the written word with the idea it represents, they are well on their way to becoming strong readers and writers.

Too often, however, word walls feature common sight words that hold no real allure for the young child developing an interest in literacy. Children might memorize the words *I* and *you* and can rattle them off when they are pointed to, but these words do not excite them or motivate them to engage with the printed words the wall highlights. As with the charts just discussed, children are much more likely to engage with a word wall if it is placed where they can see it and if they have a role in creating it.

Making a word wall part of your regular routine can greatly enhance children's engagement with the tool. You can make the task of adding to a word wall one of the daily jobs children do in the classroom. Just like there are jobs for line leader and pet feeder, one child's job can be to come up with a Word of the Day for the wall as part of your morning circle time. Demonstrate writing the word on a sentence strip, helping children connect the sounds with the letters that represent them. The child who contributed the word can write her name on the sentence strip, add a picture to it, and post the word on the wall.

When children come up with words, the word wall will feature words like *Ninja Turtles* (a great opportunity to teach about capital letters in proper nouns and spaces between words), *grandma*, and *popcorn*. These words are much more likely to draw children's interest than typical sight words are. When children contribute the words, word walls become meaningful and relevant to children and they are more likely to want to read the words.

Of course, if a new word is added every day, the word wall may soon become unwieldy. You can easily solve this problem by rotating the words children add. As children take turns adding words, they can replace the words they contributed earlier with new ones. The old words can go in a box in the writing area so children can continue to refer to them throughout the year.

A WORD WALL SURPRISE

A teacher in Colorado shared a story of how her word wall became an integral part of her classroom. She had adopted the practice of having children select a Word of the Day to be added to the word wall. She watched with delight as children added words like *superhero*, *train*, *buffalo*, and *love*. She was excited to see them looking for new words and noticed children interacting more with the word wall, which had previously featured words related to the current study that she selected and was mostly ignored.

One day, a child decided that *booger* would be his submission for Word of the Day. Of course, all the children laughed with glee. At first, the teacher was a little concerned that adding the word would cause trouble with children and families, but she decided to go with it. She modeled spelling out and writing the word, provided it to the child so he could color it, and helped him post it on the wall. The kids had their giggle and then quickly got involved in the day's activities.

Throughout the day, the teacher noticed something unusual. Every time she looked in the direction of the word wall, at least two children were in front of it, running their fingers along the word *booger* and reading it. They were also pointing out other words they had contributed or that they recognized. Whenever an adult walked into the room, a child would grab her or him by the hand, take the adult to the word wall, and point out the fun new addition. While at first the teacher had been hesitant to accept the unorthodox contribution, she found that its presence on the wall was encouraging children to interact more with the words and helping build the skills and the love of language they needed to become strong readers and writers.

Classroom schedules. Classroom schedules can help children make sense of their day as well as learn sequencing and gain a better understanding of time concepts. However, when these schedules are placed out of children's view or feature generic cartoons, they just serve to add to the visual noise of the classroom.

To make these schedules meaningful, they might feature pictures of the current children in the classroom involved in the activities they do every day. Teachers can also refer to the schedule throughout the day to make it relevant and useful for children. For example, a child can derive comfort from being able to place a sticky note on the section of the schedule that shows when her grandma is coming back to pick her up. Children can also move a clothespin or sticky note from section to section to indicate their progression through the day. You can also refer to the schedule to share with children special events or points of interest that might be on the day's agenda. All these uses help make a pictorial schedule a meaningful part of children's classroom experience.

Birthday boards. Birthday boards are another aspect of classroom decor that often fade into the realm of visual noise, especially if they are placed above children's eye level and have very little relevance or meaning for them.

As with other displays, you can involve children in creating the birthday board and use pictures of them to make it more relevant and meaningful. For example, the board can feature a photo of each child holding a piece of paper showing his or her date of birth. These photos can be sorted into months (a great small-group activity) and attached to posterboard to make a meaningful, relevant birthday board. The display becomes useful when it is placed at children's eye level and you point to it when it is someone's birthday, to talk with children about how many months and days are left until their birthdays, or to talk with them about who shares a birth month or day.

As with all aspects of classroom decor, it is important to make sure that posted items are reflective of and relevant to the children who learn and play there and their families. For example, in some cultures, birthdays are not celebrated. Make sure you are aware of cultural backgrounds and preferences as you create displays for your classroom.

Take a step back periodically and look at your classroom with new eyes to evaluate the level of busyness. How many surfaces are covered with displays? How many items are hanging from the ceiling? As you scan the classroom, do you find it easy to focus on particular objects or is there perhaps too much to see? Evaluate each display, and amend or take down those that are not contributing to children's learning experiences.

Manage Crowding

It must be difficult to be a young child and to spend most of your waking hours in an environment that forces you not only to share space with others, but to share all other aspects of daily classroom life as well. Children may communicate their distress with this situation through challenging behaviors. We probably should not be surprised when children bite, hit, or push if they are constantly feeling like they have no personal space. You can lessen this sense of claustrophobia by how you set up the environment and manage the classroom.

The classroom environment should provide spaces that allow children to escape and be by themselves. See-through and mesh fabrics can help create spaces where children feel like they are isolated but supervision is still possible. These retreats provide a place where children can not only avoid the hustle and bustle of the classroom, but also find a private space to relax and recharge away from others. These pockets of solitude are especially important for children who are introverts, and as teachers, we need to recognize that not all children benefit or draw energy from continuous contact with other people.

You can also minimize children's experience of being in a crowd by how you manage the classroom. Often in a classroom, teachers resort to a herding instinct, moving children as a group from one area or activity to the next. This especially can be true in toddler classrooms. For example, you may plan an art experience and have all children sit at a table to participate in the activity. After art, you bring the children together to the carpet for a movement game. When children spend most of their time in a group, two things can happen that contribute to challenging behaviors: children may feel crowded and they may feel they lack choice in how they spend their time. Hence, they often act out in response to their powerlessness. (You will find more on this in factor 8 on page 43.)

You can combat crowding by limiting how much time children spend in large groups. Most experiences should be planned for small groups, and children should have autonomy to move through experiences and areas of the classroom as their interests dictate. You can facilitate these small-group experiences during free choice time. Additionally, you can make sure classroom centers are interesting and fresh by incorporating enhancements (see **figure 1.3** on page 38 for enhancement ideas). Children can choose if they want to join in the small-group activity or if they prefer to play in one of the classroom learning centers. Your role is to get children started on the activity, and then rotate around the room, having conversations with them to understand their experiences and enhance their learning. Not only will small groups and individual interactions minimize crowding, these teaching strategies are also more conducive to true learning.

Adjust Height

In Times Square, buildings and billboards tower over the crowds below, contributing to a sense of feeling small, powerless, or lost. Often, in early childhood classrooms, tall ceilings, cabinets, displays, and people (adults) can create these same feelings in young children. You can remedy this by bringing displays down to children's level and limiting the amount of tall cabinets and furniture as much as possible. You can also lessen children's sense of smallness by using fabric or other materials to create cubbyholes and spaces that are at children's height. These little areas of the classroom will provide a space for children to escape the often overpowering height of the adult world.

Another idea is to have the adults in the room lower themselves to children's level. This might mean crouching, having seating options around the classroom, or sitting on the floor while interacting with children. This simple practice significantly changes the sense of height in a classroom.

Figure 1.3 Enhancement Ideas for Classroom Centers

Note: These ideas are meant to supplement the staple materials you already have available in your centers, such as books related to the topic. Also, always check your licensing regulations, allergy information, and safety-based age restrictions before introducing new materials into the classroom.

CENTER	ENHANCEMENT IDEAS
Pretend play	Create a variety of prop boxes. (Share these lists of materials with families. You will be amazed by what they contribute to make prop boxes.)
	Fabric: leftover fabric pieces from sewing, remnants from fabric stores, cut-up towels or sheets
	Shoe store: shoes, cash register, shoe boxes, bags, rulers for measuring (change out the shoes for clothes, groceries, pet supplies, and so on to make any other type of store)
	Restaurant: tables, tablecloths, menus, cash register, kitchen tools, cookbooks, food boxes, play food, aprons, dishes, pencils, notepads for taking orders
	Post office: junk mail (flyers, ads), envelopes, pencils, cardboard mailboxes, mailbags
	Pizza parlor: pizza boxes, cardboard rounds, felt pieces cut like toppings, notepads for taking orders, pencils, cash register, tables, tablecloths, phone, aprons, dishes
	Flower shop: pretend and real flowers, vases, note cards, pencils, phone, string, ribbons, pictures of floral arrangements
	Bakery/coffee shop: cookbooks, pictures of baked goods, play food, cookie sheets, cardboard oven, phone, cash register, coffee machine, dishes
	Laundromat: washers and dryers made from boxes, empty containers of laundry soap, clothes, laundry baskets
	Submarine/train/airplane: pictures of landscapes (as viewed through the vehicle's windows), chairs arranged in rows, tickets, appropriate clothing, dishes, trays, play food, pillows, blankets
	TV screen/theater stage: large piece of cardboard with the center cut out to look like a screen or stage, clothing, puppets, paper, crayons and markers, masks, other props as needed
	Movie theater: seating, sheet hung as a screen, food boxes and containers for concession stand, tickets, paper 3-D glasses (this can easily be adapted for a sporting event as well)
	Farm/garden: seed packets, yard tools, gardening books, play fruits and vegetables, sheets to use as garden beds, baskets for harvesting crops, cardboard stand for selling the harvest
	Science lab: beakers, cups, measuring tools, lab coats, goggles, liquids and other materials for children to mix and experiment with, pencils, notepads, child-safe microscope
	Doctor/dentist/optometrist/vet: seating and magazines for waiting area, file folders, phone, pencils, x-rays, machines made from boxes, cots, lab coats, child-friendly tools, patients (dolls, stuffed animals), appropriate decor (eye charts, body chart, models of teeth), glasses with empty frames, fabric for bandages
	Office: phones, desks, phone books, computer keyboards and mouses, cardboard screens, file folders, paper, pencils, rulers
	Garage/repair shop: old appliances with cords removed, tools, ropes and boxes to create machines, car made from boxes
	Construction zone: hard hats, tools, pieces of cardboard, blueprints, tape, pictures of buildings
Art	Besides the staples (paints, construction paper, crayons, scissors, collage materials, child-safe glue, and markers) that should always be available, consider adding the following:
	magazines, junk mail, corks, coated wire, recycled wrapping paper, greeting cards, calendars, different types of paper (wax, sand, parchment), foil, paint sample chips, natural materials (leaves, twigs, flowers), printed paper party materials (napkins, paper plates, gift bags), different types of brushes, fabric, string, ribbon, thread, yarn, loom, beads, cardboard sheets and tubes, egg cartons, wood pieces, paper coasters, smooth tiles, siding, flooring, linoleum pieces, or child-safe mirrors
	Periodically add in interesting items, such as plates of fruit, fresh flowers, or pictures of great works of art, to inspire children's creativity. You might also make various playdoughs (cloud dough, oatmeal dough, rice dough) available to children.

Figure 1.3 Enhancement Ideas for Classroom Centers (continued)

Math/ manipulatives	Consider adding items like the following to your math center: bottle and jar tops, beads, coupons, calculators, measuring cups and spoons, phones and phone books, natural items (pine cones, rocks, sea glass, twigs), buttons, beads, any sortable items (silverware, fabric pieces, game or puzzle pieces, playing cards, paper coasters)
Writing/ language	In addition to pencils and paper, consider adding the following items to your writing center: computer keyboards and mouses, cardboard screens, many types of paper (index cards, envelopes, note cards), stencils, license plates, various writing tools (pencils, markers, pens), chalkboards and chalk, whiteboards and dry-erase markers, plastic letters, greeting cards, day planners or journals, stamps and inkpads, newspapers and magazines
Science	In your science area, you can have a sensory table always available and full of interesting items to explore, such as ice cubes with spices, food coloring, or small toys inside; flax seed; shampoos and gels; dish soap and sand mix; flavored water; essential oils; soil; aquarium pebbles; warm water; flour; beans; rice; and shredded paper. Also consider adding other materials for children to explore: owner's manuals for machines, old appliances (cords removed) for children to take apart and put back together, measuring cups and spoons, child-safe plants, animal artifacts (empty nests, hives, etc.), natural items (leaves, branches, flowers, rocks, pine cones), child-safe microscope
Blocks	You can add materials like the following to your block center: cardboard boxes, shipping containers (*tip*: make friends with a local wine store, as wine bottles are shipped in very interesting containers to keep them from breaking), fabric, string, twigs, step stools or phone books to challenge children to build at different levels, plastic cups, egg cartons, index cards and markers (to label constructions), blueprints, pictures of interesting structures, containers (plastic, cardboard, and metal)

Note: This is by no means an exhaustive list, but is meant to inspire your own ideas of materials you might add to centers to keep them fresh and interesting. For specific school-age enhancement ideas, refer to figure 1.2 on page 25.

Create a Sense of Warmth Using Natural Materials

Concrete, glass, and metal combine to make Times Square a cold place devoid of nature. In the same way, plastic, tile, and other shiny surfaces can create a feeling of coldness in the early childhood classroom. The intentional incorporation of nature and items of beauty into the learning environment can create a sense of warmth that embraces children and lets them know that the space in which they spend so much time welcomes them.

When you think of how to add nature into your classroom, you might first think about adding a couple of plants to the tops of shelves. While plants are important, there are many other ways nature can be incorporated throughout the classroom.

Natural and more inviting containers can replace many plastic, vinyl, or other synthetic items. Baskets, fabric containers, and metal buckets (used sparingly as too much metal can make the classroom feel shiny and cold) can be used instead of plastic bins to store materials. Bricks can be used to hold drying paintbrushes or writing materials. Secondhand stores are a great source for interesting bins that will add textural and visual interest to the learning environment. Classroom shelves take on sensory interest and a sense of warmth when plastic bins disappear.

Soft fabrics or woven mats can be placed on shelves and tables to mask the shiny surfaces that reflect light and contribute to a sense of coldness.

Natural fabric pieces can replace store-bought pretend play clothing, which is often stiff and made from synthetic materials. Besides adding warmth, these materials will feel better to wear and can greatly contribute to the creativity of children's play. A store-bought vest decorated to look like a mail carrier's uniform can only really be used for one role, that of a mail carrier. But a long piece of fabric is open-ended. It can be a superhero's cape, an ancient emperor's toga, an African princess's headdress, or a mail carrier's jacket. Children will craft the clothing they need for the characters they are playing in that moment.

In addition, providing fabric pieces for dress-up, as opposed to gender-normed pretend play clothing, can alleviate the tension some adults experience around children dressing up in items that represent atypical gender roles (boys putting on tutus or girls wearing ties). With neutral materials, there are no preconceived notions about how children wear certain items of clothing.

Natural artifacts can also replace some of the learning materials in the classroom. Sorting seashells, sea glass, or rocks is equal in learning value to sorting plastic counting bears. Building with twigs or wood pieces challenges children's understanding of balance and gravity in the same way building with plastic planks or blocks does. Pine cones, leaves, rocks, and other items children can find in parks or in their backyards are much more interesting to study than the plastic dinosaurs or resin-covered specimens often found in science centers. Look for creative ways to swap out bright plastic classroom materials for artifacts from nature to help create an inviting experience for children.

Elements of natural beauty can also warm up the classroom and help create welcoming spaces. Small indoor water fountains provide calming sounds and auditory interest. Incorporating essential oils into the water will add calming scents (provided the children in the classroom can tolerate scents). Wood-framed pieces of art can soften a harsh cement wall space. Throw rugs add sensory interest while defining classroom spaces. Wind chimes made from natural items create soothing sounds while adding visual interest. Adults devote lots of creative energy to making their living spaces retreats of comfort, warmth, and beauty. That same energy can be applied to building learning environments that send the message to children that they are welcomed and worthy of beauty.

Decrease Noise

The noise of Times Square can feel overwhelming and confusing. Likewise, when a high level of noise overtakes the early childhood classroom, it can lead children to behave in challenging ways. Children will speak louder to compete with the ambient noise, and in frustration, teachers often repeat reminders to "use inside voices." A high level of noise can compel children to increased levels of activity. And children who are overwhelmed by noise may strike out against others or break down in tears of frustration.

Many of the strategies discussed previously can cut down on classroom noise as well:

- Using fabric to add beauty or create lower spaces for children can also dampen the sounds of the classroom.

- A small water feature can incorporate nature and warmth, as well as provide soothing background sounds.

- By reducing classroom crowding, children are more likely to engage in conversations with others right next to them instead of trying to talk to or over the whole group.

- One final strategy is to play music in the classroom only as part of an activity or when children initiate it. Constant background music, especially upbeat music, often just adds to the noise level of the classroom. Children will raise their voices to compete with it.

Our environments are constantly sending messages about how we should behave in them. You may notice that hotel rooms feature soft colors and lighting—the message is that this is a place for relaxation and rest. The chaos of Times Square excites people and can compel them to behave in ways they might not in their everyday lives. When classrooms are like Times Square, all the elements discussed can come together to rev up children and overwhelm them. When children feel overwhelmed, they may communicate it through challenging behaviors. In the garden that is the early childhood classroom, removing Times Square–like elements will lead to an environment that is more conducive to all children thriving.

STRATEGIES FOR QUIETLY GAINING CHILDREN'S ATTENTION

When the classroom gets noisy, you can use creative games and activities to gain children's attention instead of raising your own voice. Try some of the following strategies:

- Whisper when you want children to listen; they will have to stop talking to hear what you are saying.

- Start a chant such as, "When I say *listen*, you say *up*." You say, "Listen." And children respond, "Up." Repeat until all children are paying attention and chanting with you. Another chant you can use is, "If you can hear my voice, put your hands on your head." Continue, naming different body parts to touch, until all children are participating.

- You can also use props to get children's attention. Children can learn that when you wave a towel or put on a certain hat, it is time to stop and listen.

- Finally, you can play games to get children's attention. Saying "freeze" and standing like a statue can get many children to stop and play along. After a few seconds, say "unfreeze" and move with energy until you say "freeze" again. When all children are playing the game, you can communicate what you need to say.

Factor 6: Temptations

"Childhood is a state of mind which ends the moment a puddle is first viewed as an obstacle instead of an opportunity."—Unknown

Children spend a lot of time hearing "no." When children face a constant barrage of hearing what they cannot do, they can develop feelings of powerlessness and frustration. Those feelings may be communicated through challenging behaviors. Early childhood classrooms should be designed to reduce the need for the word *no*.

Anything within children's reach should be okay for them to touch. Teacher desks have no place in an early childhood classroom. When possible, remove them. Store special or teacher-only materials on high shelves where children cannot see or touch them. The same is true for containers that hold items that are not appropriate for little hands.

Children are naturally curious and lack impulse control. It is not reasonable to expect that they follow a long list of rules for what they can and cannot touch or interact with. Limiting temptations to engage with unsafe objects in the classroom sets up children for success. There are fewer opportunities for them to get in trouble when items they should not touch are removed from their environment as much as possible.

It may be impossible to remove all temptations from a classroom, especially when different age groups share the space. Whenever possible, add physical reminders to help children know what they can and cannot touch. A sheet over a shelf reminds children that whatever is behind it is off limits. These barriers are even more effective when they provide an alternative for children's use. For example, a piece of cardboard placed in front of a bookshelf containing inappropriate materials can provide a visual reminder of expectations. When you also place a basket of markers near the cardboard, you provide children with the alternative to color on the cardboard (instead of playing with what is behind it). You might also use felt as a shelf covering and provide children with felt pieces from their favorite stories, or use a wooden garden trellis and provide pieces of fabric for children to weave into it. One enterprising director poked holes in a large piece of Styrofoam, painted a bunch of corks that fit in the holes, and used her giant pegboard to block off cots that needed to be stored in the classroom.

Overall, in limiting children's access to some materials, the most important strategy in avoiding challenging behaviors is to make sure you have plenty of appropriate materials for children to use instead. When they are engaged with fun and interesting materials, they are less likely to focus on the materials they cannot touch. This approach has the bonus of making your job a little less stressful by decreasing how often you must correct children's behavior and say "no." Hence, you have more time and energy to engage in positive interactions with children focused around what they *can* do.

Factor 7: Physical Development Needs

"Sensible children always run. Walking is slower and not much fun."
—Unknown

Young children's bodies develop at incredible rates. It seems like almost overnight a child goes from mastering holding up his head to dashing up and down the stairs. There is nothing more fun than showing off a new physical skill or practicing a new way to control or use a body part. Yet in many cases, we keep children inside much of the day, enclosed in walls with many other children where "walking feet" and "inside voices" are the rule.

Children are naturally compelled to practice their new physical skills and exercise their developing muscles. When classrooms do not provide an outlet for this need, challenging behaviors will often result. The skills themselves are not problematic. However, the ways children exercise those skills can result in dangerous situations. For example, throwing is not a challenging behavior, but throwing blocks or chairs is. Climbing is not a challenging behavior, but climbing on shelves is. Running is not a challenging behavior, but running in a classroom crowded with furniture and other children is. The trick is to find ways children can safely display and hone these skills.

Often, classrooms relegate physical skills to outside where children have more room and fewer obstacles. But outside time is often severely limited, and in many regions, days or weeks pass during which children cannot go outside due to weather conditions. After five snow days in a row, when a child's body is screaming, "Run! Run! Run!" and a teacher is saying, "Walking feet," something is going to give. Most likely, a child's need to move will win out.

To decrease challenging behaviors due to this factor, you can provide safe ways for kids to practice these physical skills in the classroom. **Figure 1.4** on page 44 provides some ideas.

You may be concerned that allowing children to engage in these behaviors in the classroom may make the behaviors *more* prevalent. Instead, you are providing safe outlets for behaviors children are going to do anyway. When children are redirected to these safe alternatives, injuries and challenging behaviors related to this factor become less likely.

Factor 8: Opportunity for Choice and Power

"Children are like wet cement. Whatever falls on them makes an impression."—Dr. Haim Ginott

Having a sense of power in one's life is a deep human need. People strike out when they feel powerless, and young children are not immune to this need. There is not much power in being a child. Generally, you are told what to wear,

Figure 1.4 Classroom Enhancements to Accommodate Physical Behaviors

BEHAVIOR	CLASSROOM ENHANCEMENTS
Throwing	• Sticky paper on wall and paper balls • Target on wall and tape balls • Box mounted on wall and paper balls • Basket and rolled-up socks • Soft balls with boxes as targets
Kicking and hitting	• Large pillow • Beach ball suspended from ceiling
Climbing	• Boxes and pillows to climb over and through • Small climbing structure • Step stool
Running	• A picture of a treadmill control panel, a timer, and a taped rectangle on the floor as a pretend treadmill where children can run in place • A taped track in the hallway
Tearing	• Bucket full of paper scraps • Small flyers, phone books, or advertising bundles
Dumping	• Large bin or wading pool with various manipulatives and buckets • Water and a collection of cups and sponges
General large muscle outlets	• 2-liter bottles filled with water to shake and lift • Exercise stations placed around the classroom • Taped squares to jump in or from one to the other

what and when to eat, where and when to sleep and move from one place to another, and what to do. At times, when a child feels especially powerless, she will express this need through tantrums, defiance, or hurting others. When you provide opportunities for children to choose or have power in the classroom, challenging behaviors related to this factor will be reduced.

Examples of Opportunities for Choice and Power

Providing opportunities for choice and power does not mean that you stand back and let children do whatever they want without interference. It means that the classroom and daily structure provide chances for children to make choices about how they use materials and spend their time.

Provide two options. A child's sense of power might come from having the ability to choose between two acceptable options you provide. For example, "Let's get this block center cleaned up. Do you want to hand me the blocks, or do you want me to hand them to you?" or, "Time to go outside. Are you going to put your hat or boots on first?" Neither of these choices really impact the expected outcome of the situation, but the child feels like he has some power.

Give a choice of materials and how to use them. You can also cultivate a child's sense of power by giving her the ability to access materials and choose how to use them. This means that, throughout the day, children have lots of time to enter and leave learning centers as they please. In those centers, they can pick the materials they want from low shelves and use those materials in a variety of ways. We see this in action when children can go into the art center and pick a magazine, some glue, some yarn, or other materials and use them to make a collage instead of having to complete a project the teacher selected for the day.

Practice family-style dining. Family-style dining can also be a wonderful strategy to build a sense of empowerment in young children. As children serve themselves, they are making choices about what and how much food they put on their plates. Not only are they more likely to eat the foods they choose, they are less likely to strike out against the feeling that they are powerless about a basic human need. Family-style dining often encourages calm and enjoyable meals during which children can talk with teachers and each other.

Give students input into the course of study. Children also feel a sense of power when they help determine the course of study for the class. Instead of basing themes on a calendar or a predetermined schedule, you can tap into children's interests to plan classroom activities. Maybe many children are talking about the newest movie—enlist them in turning your pretend play area into the setting of that film. Perhaps children are enamored of the roadwork happening in front of the school. Set aside the preplanned theme of "on the farm" and instead dive into a study about construction.

Include students in lesson planning. You can also integrate choice by regularly including children in curriculum planning. Once or twice a week, one of your classroom jobs for children can be picking a book for storytime, choosing a way to move when transitioning to the playground, or selecting the song everyone will sing at group time. Such simple tasks can make children feel like they have some power in how they spend their time in the classroom.

Avoid Giving Fake Choices

While it is important that you look for opportunities to instill choice into the classroom environment, it is equally important not to present fake choices. When you end statements with the question "Okay?" or start a sentence with "Are you ready to . . . " you are giving children the idea that there is a choice when, most likely, there is none. Instead, state expectations clearly and succinctly, weaving in choice when available.

For example, instead of, "It's time to clean up, okay?" a concise, "It is cleanup time. Who is starting in the block center, and who is tackling the pretend play center?" sends the message that helping with cleanup is not a choice. Likewise, the question, "Are you ready to get on your cot?" conveys the message that the child has the right to say, "No, in fact I am not ready to lie on my cot at this minute." Instead you can weave in choice for a child who struggles with naptime by saying, "Time for nap. Do you want your cot next to the window or in the library?" In both instances, the child feels like he has some power in the situation even as he complies with the expectation.

In our society, we often see how people strike out when they feel powerless. Some challenging behaviors in the classroom are the result of a similar struggle for children. When teachers seek to empower children, as opposed to breaking their wills, challenging behaviors related to this factor will begin to disappear.

Factor 9: Clarity of Expectations

"If you have told a child a thousand times and he still does not understand, then it is not the child who is the slow learner."—Walter Barbee

Sometimes it is not that children are exhibiting challenging behaviors; it is that they do not understand what is expected of them. As adults, we understand many social expectations based on our years of experience. Children do not have the benefit of those years of experience, and unless teachers define an expectation, they may not have the knowledge to comply.

There also may be times when a behavioral expectation at school is very different from one at home. Unless teachers clearly explain what they expect children to do, it is not fair to assume that children will automatically understand and comply.

For example, classroom mealtimes usually involve staying in one's seat throughout the meal, eating from one's own plate, serving oneself or asking for more, and clearing one's plate when finished. At home, mealtimes may be completely different. A child may eat dinner while standing at a coffee table watching TV. Many meals may be consumed in the car on the way from one activity to another. Or, a family may eat together, and the child is fed from the plates of the adults at the table. These dining behaviors are neither better nor worse than what happens at school: They are simply different.

The same can be true for rest time. Many American children go to sleep in front of a screen, either in their own beds, on a couch, or in the bed of a parent or sibling. Bedtime might mean sharing a bed with another person or going to sleep in a completely dark and silent room. In most cases, bedtime does not involve falling asleep with shoes on on a hard cot or mat in a well-lit room surrounded by other children and activity.

Make an Expectations Book

In both of the previous examples, mealtime and naptime, you can avoid challenging behaviors by clearly defining expectations. One way to do this is to make books that feature pictures of children demonstrating what it means to eat or sleep in the classroom. You can read the book at the start of the year (if applicable), periodically as children transition into the room, and with new children as they join the class. For example, the text in a book for naptime expectations might say (with one line per page of the book, plus illustrations):

- ◆ I go to the bathroom and wash my hands.
- ◆ I get my blanket and spread it out on my cot.
- ◆ I lie under the blanket on my cot.
- ◆ I stay very still and close my eyes.
- ◆ I think calm thoughts and take deep breaths.

- I have pleasant dreams until it is time to wake up.
- I wake up refreshed and ready for more fun.

Consider making books for other times of the day that prove challenging for children. Illustrate the books with photographs of children demonstrating the expected behaviors, or invite children to draw pictures. Besides mealtime and naptime, these might include arrival, circle time, and times where waiting is inevitable (such as waiting to use bathrooms in the hallway). When you define your expectations and communicate them with clear and concise words, children are more likely to be able to comply.

Factor 10: Presence of Joy

"What soap is to the body, laughter is to the soul."—Yiddish proverb

Childhood should be a time of whimsy and laughter, and it is the greatest privilege of the early childhood professional to be part of that world. Environments built on joy are those in which there will be fewer challenging behaviors. The final factor that may contribute to challenging behaviors in the classroom is a need for joy and fun.

Ways to Infuse Joy and Fun into the Classroom

There are many ways you can infuse joy and fun into the classroom:

- Share silly songs and fingerplays with children.
- Designate a space in the classroom for a weekly joke. Families can take turns sharing a joke.
- Read silly books during storytimes. Books like *King Bidgood's in the Bathtub* and *Piggies*, both by Audrey Wood, will tickle children's funny bones.
- Infuse fun into learning. Everyone says there are no words that rhyme with *orange*, but what about *jorange* and *plorange*? Combining beginning sounds with ending syllables can result in new, silly rhyming words. These nonsense words not only build phonemic awareness, but will inspire a lot of giggles.

Certain times of day often plagued by challenging behaviors—namely, cleanup time and transitions—can especially benefit from some elements of fun.

Cleanup Time

When it comes time to clean the classroom, tempers often flare as children try to avoid the responsibility of cleaning up and teachers try to coerce them into obeying. Hard as it may be to believe, cleanup time can be a breeze if you are creative in how you present it.

Pick a fun and uplifting song to indicate cleanup time. For example, in one of my classrooms, our cleanup song was "I Will Survive" by Gloria Gaynor. It played on a loop, and we sang and danced around the classroom as we cleaned. For some children, cleanup time was a favorite part of the day!

Play games to encourage children to clean up. For example, sit in a circle and name two children. Those children go as quickly as possible to pick up and put away three items, return to the circle, and tag two more children. The game continues until everything is clean.

Make cards showing different items in the classroom. During cleanup time, children pick cards to show what they should clean (for example, one card might show a picture of purses or triangle blocks). When that item is put away, the child picks another card. Children continue picking cards until everything is clean.

Lead a cleanup train. Have children line up behind you and move around the classroom. In each area pause and chant, "If you are wearing blue, blue, blue, if you are wearing blue, clean up here." Continue with different colors in different areas until the room is clean.

Play "freeze and switch cleanup." Encourage children to start cleaning. Say "freeze," and all children stop what they are doing. When you say "switch," they move to another area of the classroom and freeze. When you say "start," they start cleaning again until you say "freeze" again.

As Julie Andrews sang in *Mary Poppins*, "In every job that must be done, there is an element of fun. You find the fun and snap! The job's a game." By injecting fun into the drudgery of cleanup time, children will look forward to the task instead of looking for ways to rebel against it.

Transitions

As children and teachers navigate the school day, naturally they must transition from one activity or period to the next. As mentioned earlier, children have not yet developed self-control, so these times can be difficult. If teachers have elevated expectations for children during transitions (such as everyone must stand in a straight line and be completely quiet), these times can be especially challenging. It is best to arrange daily routines so there are as few transitions as possible. However, when transitions cannot be avoided, they can be made easier for everyone when they are fun and planned with realistic expectations. Here are some suggestions.

Find interesting ways to move from one place to another. Walking quietly in a straight line is no fun at all. But taking giant steps, hopping like kangaroos, or tiptoeing can add joy to these transitions.

Use games to get children's attention. Speaking in funny voices, leading children in silly dances, and initiating call-and-response chants are more likely to get children to listen than using an angry voice will.

Use the element of mystery to get children's attention. Hide an item in a pillow-case or bag. If there is a time children must wait, introduce the bagged item and keep children engaged by giving hints or letting them ask questions until they can guess the secret item.

Involve children in deciding how to transition between experiences. One of your daily jobs can be selecting a child to pick the songs or how to move during that day's transitions.

When you make transitions fun, children are more likely to be engaged and move smoothly from one experience to another throughout the day.

Early childhood classrooms should be places of joy and fun. The daily life of a teacher should include many smiles, laughs, and happy moments. If a teacher is not happy in the classroom, children will pick up on that, and the lack of joy will often translate into challenging behaviors. Looking for ways to incorporate fun into every day will not only make your job more enjoyable, it will make your classroom a more peaceful, cooperative place.

Analyzing Classroom Factors

When you face challenging behaviors, the first step is to look at how these ten factors might be affecting a child, especially if it seems like many challenges are occurring at the same time. If several children are exhibiting challenging behaviors, it can indicate that there are factors in your classroom contributing to the behaviors. You can use the "Classroom Factors Observation Form" on pages 163–164 in the appendix to record your observations. At times, it can be hard to look objectively at one's own classroom, so it may be helpful to have a colleague assist in identifying the root reasons for behaviors.

There may also be times when a new child enters the classroom and disrupts a routine that seemed to be working for all the other children. It could be that, for this child, one of these ten classroom factors is having an impact. Even if no other child struggles with sitting through circle time, you may need to make adjustments to meet the individual needs of the new child. Shifting your focus from "fixing" a child to finding ways for that child to be successful means that you adjust expectations or change practices to meet every child's needs.

Chapter Summary

When you pay attention to and address these ten classroom factors, you are preparing a foundation for children to be successful in your classroom. Just as a gardener meticulously prepares the ground so plants can sprout strong roots and shoot up toward the sun, a teacher prepares a classroom so young children will be more likely to thrive and their challenging behaviors will decrease.

Chapter 2

Active Learning:
Create Ideal Growing Conditions

In chapter 1, we looked at how teachers can reduce challenging behaviors by creating classroom environments that benefit children's learning and development. Like plants under the care of the determined gardener, children are more likely to thrive when a teacher is committed to cultivating ideal growing conditions. The most important step toward this goal is to create classrooms based on research that tells us how children truly learn and develop. The gardener seeks to create conditions in which plants will flourish, as opposed to trying to change the plants to meet her chosen conditions. Likewise, a teacher needs to teach how children learn, instead of trying to get children to learn how he wants to teach. Children are naturally active learners, so when teachers incorporate the tenets of active learning, fewer challenging behaviors will occur.

Think about the last time you learned something. Chances are you heard a new idea or new way of doing something and decided that it was interesting or might be helpful. As exciting as the new idea might have been, your true learning most likely came as you worked through it. This may have happened through conversing with a colleague, honing your skills while putting the new idea into practice, or diving in and investigating the idea.

As humans, we do not typically learn by sitting still and listening to others. For most of us, after a few minutes of listening to a lecture or sitting still, we either zone out or look for ways to engage our brains and hands—for example, checking a phone, doodling, or talking with a neighbor. This is especially true of children, who have not yet developed the self-regulation skills needed to sit quietly and pay attention for a significant period of time. Like many adults, real learning happens for children when they can actively engage with new ideas. Active learning occurs when teachers plan experiences around presenting content in a way that provides children opportunities to use their brains and bodies to explore interesting concepts.

With increased focus on children's academic performance at younger ages, teachers sometimes lean on inappropriate teaching methods to meet those demands. When classroom instruction is built around practices such as flash cards, worksheets, lots of sitting, and other developmentally unsuitable approaches, children are prone to react to these stifling conditions with challenging behaviors. Through these behaviors, they are communicating that the instruction and learning activities are not designed around how they learn best. To truly support children's learning and development, you must focus as much on *how* you teach as on what you teach. Building early childhood classrooms around *active learning* is one of the most powerful tools for preventing and reducing problem behaviors.

A DIET OF BIRTHDAY CAKE

Often when teachers are planning learning experiences, they may base the experience on something they saw on Pinterest or plan an activity because it reflects the current theme in a way that will result in a "cute" project. While these projects are planned with the best of intentions, they often do not result in true learning for children. To understand how this approach to lesson planning is not helpful for children, let's look at the example of birthday cake. Birthday cake is wonderful to look at and even more fun to eat. However, we all know that while birthday cake is a special treat to be enjoyed periodically, a body does not get what it needs nutritionally by eating a diet of birthday cake.

In the same way, a reliance on fun, attractive projects in the classroom does not provide children's brains with what they need to thrive. Active learning provides children's brains with the nutrition that leads to true learning and long-term critical-thinking and creative problem-solving skills. Teacher-directed "birthday cake" projects can be an interesting and periodic add-on in a classroom that is designed primarily around active learning.

The opposite of active learning is, of course, passive learning. If you expect children to remain passive recipients of teaching, instead of being actively involved in the learning process, challenging behaviors will often result. Young students being actively involved in the learning process not only leads to fewer behavior challenges, but also fosters deep, authentic learning that provides a solid foundation for the lifelong skills they will need to compete in a global workforce.

Designing HOMES for Active Learning

Even if you are unfamiliar with the term *active learning*, it is easy to identify in action. When trying to determine if a learning environment or experience is built around active learning, use the acronym HOMES:

- ◆ H = Hands-on
- ◆ O = Open-ended
- ◆ M = Meaningful
- ◆ E = Engaging
- ◆ S = Sensory-oriented

To truly understand active learning, let's look at each of these aspects individually.

H Is for Hands-On

Young children are concrete learners. They learn better when they can touch and manipulate real objects. These real objects allow them to create a sort of "folder" system in their brains in which they can store new information. The more real materials you provide children to manipulate and explore, the more experiences they gain about the world around them, the more "folders" they create, and the more you prepare them to build on that knowledge as they move into the world of formalized learning.

When I was a teacher, I took my children on a field trip to the apple orchard. The guide invited children to pick an apple from the tree and put it in their pockets to take home. Our next stop was a hayride through the orchard. Of course, instead of saving their apples for home, the children pulled them out of their pockets and started eating them. Our bumpy ride was punctuated with lots of crunching sounds. Suddenly, from the back of the wagon, Stephanie's voice joyfully rang out, "Ms. Michelle, my apple has juice in it!" She had never before had the opportunity to bite into an apple. Because of her hands-on (and teeth-in) experience with a real apple, her concept of *apple* was that much richer. Moving forward, when Stephanie was presented with a plastic apple, a picture of an apple, or the word *apple*, she could build on her foundational understanding of a real apple to make more sense of these representations.

If real objects aren't available, have pictures or lifelike replicas in your classroom so children can gain a true sense of the world around them. We do children a disservice when we "cutesy" things up and paint a cartoon world for them. A friend of mine told me a story that perfectly illustrates this point. He was taking his four-year-old son to visit an aquarium. On the way, they were talking about the creatures they might see, and the conversation turned to the possibility of viewing an octopus. Suddenly, the young boy went quiet and his face turned pensive. After a minute, he asked, "Dad, how does the octopus keep his hat on if he lives underwater?" It turned out that the only picture of an octopus the boy had seen was the blue cartoon one with a hat that is featured on many store-bought alphabet charts. If this is the only model provided, children can indeed come to believe that the ocean is full of smiling, blue octopuses wearing fancy hats.

I came across another real-world example of hands-on learning while listening to a podcast. One of the hosts was recounting an anecdote about a test she took in first grade. A question asked how many legs a rabbit has. She wrote *two*, as all the pictures she had seen of rabbits were cartoon depictions, such as the Easter Bunny or Bugs Bunny, in which rabbits stand on their hind legs and hold things or do tasks with their front limbs (presumably arms). Until she was seven, this little girl had not been introduced to a true image of a rabbit, and this skewed her worldview.

As early childhood educators, it is our role to support children as they strive to make sense of their world. We do this by providing them with real materials or lifelike representations they can manipulate and explore.

O Is for Open-Ended

Open-ended experiences or questions are those that do not have just one right answer or result. They require children to think through possibilities, create and test hypotheses, and explore how things change and interact when used in different ways. When children are not limited in how they can use materials, you open up to them the possibility to discover something completely new.

For example, art experiences that are product-focused, in which every child's work resembles others', are close-ended. The focus is on what children are supposed to produce instead of on the process they use to make their creations. This does not allow children to be creative, express their individuality, or learn from their experiences. Every child is given, for example, the same owl cutout, two precut eyes, and six precut feathers. Even if children are allowed to put the eyes and feathers wherever they want, their creativity, critical thinking, and problem-solving are limited, if not completely eliminated, in these sorts of experiences. Instead, when you make available a variety of art materials and send the message, "I wonder what you can do with this," you give children the opportunity to be surprised by the unexpected.

The following questions can help you identify if a planned activity is close- or open-ended:

- Is there a specific end product in mind? (For example, "Today we are going to make a _____.")
- Will the final products all look similar?
- Will the final product reflect a teacher's idea or theme?
- Are children expected to use materials in the same way?
- Is the goal of the project to make something adults might immediately call "cute" or "adorable"?

If you can answer "yes" to any of these questions, the planned activity is likely focused on the end product, which makes it close-ended and, thus, not active learning.

When asked, most teachers will say that the goals of art experiences for young children are self-expression and to build creativity. However, when children are presented with models to emulate, they engage in neither. For this reason, in the active learning classroom, art is not a time of day. Instead, it is an art center stocked with interesting materials that inspire children to explore and create.

For one study, researchers created a special toy. It was a ball with four arms. Each arm had a special feature.[10] With some children, a teacher presented the ball to them by pulling one arm to make it squeak. "I found this ball and look what I can make it do," she said while pulling the arm. With other children, the teacher presented them the ball by saying, "I found this ball. I wonder what it does." Children in the first group all made the ball squeak and explored no further, quickly losing interest. Children in the second group explored the ball for much longer, had much richer language exchanges, and discovered all of the ball's hidden features.

When we give children open-ended opportunities to explore, we give them permission to discover, and discovery is the root of true learning.

M Is for Meaningful

Children are egocentric: Their ability to see the world from another's point of view has not yet developed. Child development expert Jean Piaget introduced this idea of egocentrism. He created situations in which children were asked to indicate how a mountain scene might appear from another person's perspective. The children were consistently unable to complete this task. Instead, they appeared to believe that the other person would see the mountain in the same way they did. More-recent studies have shown that perhaps Piaget's results were due more to the task being beyond children's cognitive ability than to egocentrism. Regardless, further studies have shown that the ability to set aside their own feelings, beliefs, and understandings to take on those of another is indeed limited in young children. Children are very rooted in their own realities and their behaviors and understandings of the world reflect this.

Because of this egocentrism, a learning experience is much more powerful when you can connect it to something that is of interest to children. Again, you can expend a lot of energy trying to get children interested in what you want to teach. Or, you can figure out what *they* are interested in and build learning around those interests.

If a child is interested in dogs, for instance, you can focus on literacy by reading stories about dogs, making up names for dogs, and learning and writing about dog breeds. If a child is intrigued by gardening, you can teach her math by counting how many seeds get planted in a garden, making a chart to see how long it takes a seed to sprout, and measuring various plants or how many cups of salad result from a single head of lettuce. When you plan instruction around children's interests, as opposed to a set of predetermined themes or the calendar, you build learning experiences that are much richer and more engaging to children.

> Lawrence was a four-year-old boy in Ms. Jalia's class who was fascinated by cars. He often stood at the playground fence and named the make and model of all the cars that streamed by the school. Ms. Jalia reflected his interest by bringing in car magazines and books for him. Together, they cut out pictures of the cars, glued them to paper, and recorded what he knew about each car next to the picture. By looking at these pictures and connecting them with the words, Lawrence began to read at a very young age.

Of course, the goal is not to get children reading at younger ages. In Lawrence's case, the teachers built on his natural interest, and early reading was the result. As with many other behaviors (such as walking and talking), children will read when they are developmentally ready and with the support of caring adults. A child who reads at an early age does not necessarily have an advantage over one who reads later. While it is not developmentally appropriate to expect a four-year-old to read, the learning environment Ms. Jalia created is a great illustration of how meaningful learning opportunities connected to Lawrence's interests made him want to make sense of the letters and sounds and gain more information about his passion.

E Is for Engaging

True learning happens when we engage children's minds *and* bodies. Piaget concluded that young children are sensory-motor learners. They process information as they move. While the sensory-motor stage of development typically ends around the second year of life, moving into the preoperational stage, children still need lots of opportunities to use their bodies while learning. As early childhood educator Bev Bos said, "If it hasn't been in the hand and the body, it can't be in the brain." Look for ways to help children use their bodies in the learning process. This might mean making themselves comfortable on a cushion during storytime, squeezing a sensory ball during circle time, or standing around a table during an activity instead of sitting in a chair. When children's bodies are engaged, their brains can better focus on the learning at hand.

Children also learn best when you give them interesting questions to think about and real problems to solve—in short, when you engage their brains. Yet so often, we ask children questions to which they already know the answers. For example, "What color is that ball?" "What sound does that letter make?" "How many blocks are there?" These questions do not require real thought, only that children memorize and spit back information.

In active learning experiences, you provide children with materials and activities that give them opportunities to really think. If children are going to solve the complex problems of the future, they need to be thinkers, not just memorizers. Lilian Katz, a pioneer in early childhood, makes the distinction between academic goals and cognitive goals. She contends that we overestimate children academically and underestimate them cognitively.[11] We ask children to complete academic tasks that may be beyond their ability (for example, reading fluently and with meaning by the end of kindergarten), yet continually ask them questions that stimulate no cognitive growth—just memorization or repetition of discrete pieces of knowledge. Active learning experiences are those that focus on engaging children's minds in the exercise of answering interesting questions and solving intriguing problems. For example:

- What do you think will happen next?
- How did that happen?
- What can you do with that?
- How else could you use that?
- How would you solve that problem?
- What could you do differently?
- What do you think?
- How is that the same? How is it different?
- Did you get the result you expected?

Experts worry that children who are pressured into academic tasks too early (before their brains are ready) suffer not only academically, but socially and emotionally as well. Instead, if we as educators spend the first few years of children's lives introducing important concepts (math, literacy, science) through experiences built around active learning, our children will be much more likely to be able to use their brains critically and creatively at each step of their schooling. One long-term, ongoing study shows the benefits of doing this continue, and even grow, as children (now adults) enter their forties and beyond.[12]

S Is for Sensory-Oriented

As sensory-motor learners, not only do children learn as they move their bodies through the world, they also learn as they use their senses to explore it. And while, around the age of two, children move from the sensory-motor to the preoperational stage in Piaget's theory of development, they still learn as their senses are engaged while moving through the world. Our senses are the only way we take in information about our environment. Think back to your childhood. How many of your most vivid memories are tied to a sensory experience? Richard Louv, author of *Last Child in the Woods*, has made the frightening claim that we are raising a generation of children who will only remember the smell and feel of plastic.[13] When you look around your classroom, try to see it from the point of view of the children you care for. What is there that is interesting for a two-year-old boy to listen to? What is there that is fascinating for an eight-year-old girl to gaze upon? Is there anything in the space in which four-year-old children spend eight hours a day that is marvelous to touch? In short, what do you have to engage children's senses?

On this topic, it is important to make the distinction between sensory *interest* and sensory *overload*, as discussed in the section on Times Square classrooms in chapter 1. That is why classrooms need to balance a neutral palette and moderate noise level with pockets of high sensory interest. When children explore through their senses, their brains create new connections as well as strengthening existing ones. These neural connections, called synapses, are what support a child in creating a deeper and more complex understanding of the world.[14] **Figure 2.1** shows specific ideas for classroom materials that stimulate all five senses, thus triggering synaptic connections.

Active learning happens when teachers intentionally plan activities, spaces, and interactions that provide children with opportunities to explore real, interesting materials in ways that are open-ended and engaging. The five HOMES factors just outlined come together to create active learning.

Figure 2.1 Classroom Materials That Stimulate the Five Senses

Note: Always be aware of your state or provincial regulations and children's allergies. Also be aware of how children react to sensory stimulation, particularly those with sensory processing challenges, and adjust to meet their individual needs.

SIGHT	HEARING	TOUCH	SMELL	TASTE
Prisms	Suspended nuts and bolts	Tree stumps	Herbs and spices	Unusual fruits or vegetables
Wind socks	Water feature	Flax seed	Potpourri or essential oils	Cooking projects
Light table or overhead projector and accessories	Wind chimes	Textured playdough	Fresh-cut wood	Herbs and spices
Optical illusion drawings or models	Pots and pans mounted on a playground fence	Natural fibers	Dried or fresh flowers	Dried and fresh fruits
Colorful fabrics from around the world	Musical instruments	Variety of brushes	Fresh fruits and vegetables	Sweets from around the world

---

Challenging Behaviors Resulting from a Lack of Active Learning

Building programs around how actively children learn is one of the most powerful steps you can take to reduce challenging behaviors. When their hands and brains are *not* engaged in real and interesting learning, children will find their own methods to remedy their disengagement. More often than not, teachers will not approve of their methods. For example, a preschool child, frustrated by having to sit at a table waiting for lunch to be served, may express that frustration by throwing his plate. A young girl, bored while waiting for each child to recite the alphabet during circle time, may seek to add some excitement by pinching the child next to her. Both of these behaviors result not from a child deliberately choosing to misbehave but from a child seeking an outlet for her natural drive to be engaged. There are times when children may be distracted or out of sorts even in the most engaging of environments. However, when teachers create active learning environments, these instances are less likely.

When childhood is honored and supported by developmentally appropriate active learning, children will need fewer challenging behaviors to communicate their frustration with boring settings and unrealistic demands. This will free you up to spend quality teaching time with children, building relationships and leading engaging and meaningful learning experiences. Active learning classrooms are those that hum with an energy of excitement and wonder instead of the constant chaotic disruptions of challenging behaviors.

The HOMES Active Learning Scale

To begin building active learning experiences, think of the HOMES acronym as a scale, with each letter worth 1 point. As you are planning experiences, measure them on this scale. While it is not realistic that all experiences score a 5, try to ensure that the experiences you plan and the spaces you create score at least a 3. **Figure 2.2** on page 60 shows three activities planned by teachers, rating ½, 3, and 5 points on the HOMES scale. A blank reproducible HOMES scale is provided on page 162 of the appendix.

While it is unrealistic to expect that all activities score a 5 on the HOMES scale, it is better for children and reduces challenging behavior when teachers strive to plan and facilitate ones that score at least 3 points. When classroom experiences are built around the idea of active learning, teachers are less likely to see challenging behaviors related to children's frustration at feeling unsuccessful, lack of engagement due to passive learning, and boredom. Along with a more peaceful classroom, teachers will see deeper learning and more engaged children when experiences are active.

Let's look at how teachers can reshape some common classroom practices by integrating elements of active learning.

Creating Active Art Experiences and Circle Times

Infusing your classroom with active learning is a powerful strategy that improves the environment for all children and proactively reduces incidents of challenging behavior, as opposed to responding to specific challenging behaviors. Two components of your classroom can especially benefit from an active learning overhaul: art experiences and circle times.

Art Projects vs. Art Experiences

The HOMES scale gives us a new lens through which to view the art projects versus art experiences debate. Art projects have been a staple in the early childhood classroom for many years in spite of numerous articles on why they are not appropriate. And with the advent of resources like Pinterest,

Figure 2.2 HOMES Active Learning Scale: Sample Experiences

Activity A

Mr. Jeremy always does a circus theme in March. For art, he has the children sit down at a table and lets each one choose a clown face that he has prepared. He provides each child with a nose, a hat, and a clown mouth to add to the face. Mr. Jeremy talks with the children about what they are making while sitting with them at the table. This activity is scored on the following scale:

Hands-on	Open-ended	Meaningful	Engaging	Sensory-oriented
Children are not working with real materials. The paper clowns are not true representations of real people that further children's understanding.	There is an end product in mind, and children follow a predetermined idea or model.	Some children may be interested in the circus once it is introduced, but the experience is not connected to children's lives unless the circus is in town and they have expressed interest in it.	No real critical thinking, creativity, or problem-solving is required for the activity. Children are using neither their brains nor their bodies.	There is nothing interesting for children to see, hear, smell, feel, or taste.
0 points	0 points	½ point	0 points	0 points

Total Score: For some children, this activity scores *maybe* ½ point on the HOMES scale.

Activity B

Ms. Britney wants her children to learn about the letter *S*. She has all children sit at the tables and provides them each a stencil of an *S* and a ball of playdough. She shows them how to roll out the playdough and press it into the stencil. This activity is scored on the following scale:

Hands-on	Open-ended	Meaningful	Engaging	Sensory-oriented
Children have a hands-on experience of shaping the letter as they form the playdough into the *S* stencil.	Children were all given the same stencil and had no opportunity to make choices about how to use the materials.	This activity did not reflect children's interests, and the teacher did not try to connect it to their experiences.	Children who were interested did use critical-thinking and problem-solving skills as they tried to form the playdough into the letter.	Children's senses of touch, smell, and sight were engaged as they used the playdough.
1 point	0 points	0 points	1 point	1 point

Total Score: This activity scores 3 points on the HOMES scale. This activity could have been a 5 with some simple modifications. As a small-group experience or center enhancement, children could choose if they wanted to participate instead of all being required to sit and do the same thing. Instead of giving each child the same stencil, Ms. Britney could have provided a variety of letter or shape stencils. This would have made the experience more open-ended and meaningful as children could choose how to use the materials. As Ms. Britney talked with them about the different letters, she could have helped them compare and contrast the letters to build a deeper understanding of letter shapes.

Activity C

Ms. Munaza notices her children have been interested in the leaves falling on the playground. She gathers leaves from her home and center and invites families to send some in. She places leaves in a bin on a table along with paper, crayons, tape, and magnifying glasses. Ms. Munaza talks with interested children about what they notice about the leaves, how they are the same, and how they differ. She invites children to draw or write about what they notice. This activity is scored on the following scale:

Hands-on	Open-ended	Meaningful	Engaging	Sensory-oriented
Children are working with real materials.	There is no predetermined model or idea of how to use the materials.	The activity is based on what the teacher notices about children's interests.	Children are using their minds to analyze objects and learn about the world. They are using their bodies as they explore the leaves.	The leaves are interesting to feel, hear, look at, and smell (and maybe even taste in some cases).
1 point	1 point	1 point	1 point	1 point

Total Score: This activity scores 5 points on the HOMES scale.

highly structured art projects have been made even more readily available and appealing to early childhood teachers. However, if you use the HOMES scale to rate these projects (see figure 2.2, activity A), it becomes evident that many of them are more for the benefit of parents or teachers than for children's learning or enjoyment. For the most part, art projects do not score more than a 1 on the HOMES scale. While these activities may not directly cause behavior challenges, they often create a classroom atmosphere where children do not have choices, cannot accomplish the prescribed task, or are not challenged physically or intellectually—all of which can contribute to challenging behaviors.

The alternative to project art is art that focuses on children's exploration of interesting materials, how those materials can be used together, and the process of creating (see **figure 2.3**). In the active learning early childhood classroom, art is not merely a time of day or a project that children complete to replicate a teacher's vision. Instead, it involves a rich art center in the classroom, time in the schedule for children to create in that center, and an attentive adult to talk with them about their creative processes.

Figure 2.3 HOMES Ideas for Active Art Experiences

In the active learning classroom, teachers encourage creativity and self-expression by adding interesting provocations to the art center to inspire children's creative processes. For example, a teacher could make an art area more interesting by incorporating any of the following materials:

Paper: Provide different sizes and shapes of paper. Also consider adding foil, sandpaper, Bubble Wrap, wax paper, newspaper, cardboard, and any other type of surface that provides a slightly different painting experience.

Brushes: Painting takes on a new twist when teachers replace regular paintbrushes with other items, such as twigs, toothbrushes, cotton swabs, wall-paint brushes, small paint rollers, and so on.

Paints: The experience of painting takes on a different dimension when teachers add different elements to the paint. They might consider adding sand, coffee grounds, scented extracts, cornstarch, flour, dish soap, or oatmeal. Anything that changes the texture, look, or smell of the paint can change the experience of painting at the easel.

Staging items: Teachers might consider sparking children's creativity by staging items that can serve as inspiration for their art. For example, posting prints of interesting paintings or drawings might motivate children to try something new. Still lifes created with flowers, play figures, or fruit and vegetables can provide models for children's painting or drawing.

3-D materials: Children also need opportunities to create three-dimensional art. Materials to provide might include corks, pipe cleaners, cardboard, spools, wood pieces, tubes, bottle caps, paper cups, twigs, and building tools.

Active vs. Passive Circle Times

A reliance on passive learning as opposed to incorporating active learning can also help explain challenging behaviors that occur during circle time. To illustrate this, consider your favorite television show. What is it you like about the show? It may be the characters or the storyline. Maybe the show keeps you in suspense, makes you laugh, or makes you feel involved in what happens. Whatever it is, you probably look forward to the show every time it airs. Now, I want you to imagine that only one episode of your favorite show is available and that you can watch only that one episode every morning for a year. As much as you like that show, you would probably tire of that one episode and would find other ways to amuse yourself while viewing it.

Now think about the circle times you host in your classroom. How often is it the same episode of the same television show every morning? For example, singing the same song, going through the calendar again, reviewing the letter of the week, and having children count to ten in Spanish. As much as children may have enjoyed parts of circle time at the start of the year, they lose their charm after being repeated over and over again. Just like you would grow bored with the same TV episode, children will grow bored when they are passive recipients of the same teaching every day. When they are bored, children will find other ways to occupy their bodies and minds, and the ways they find may manifest as challenging behaviors.

To avoid these behaviors, endeavor to make your circle times more interesting and to make them times of community building and learning. Think about how you might incorporate more active and less passive learning into them. See **figure 2.4** for ideas.

Avoiding too much repetition, however, does not mean that you have to totally reinvent the wheel every morning in circle time. What is important about your favorite TV show is that it follows the same patterns, even as the weekly storylines change and draw you in. In a similar way, your circle times should follow the same pattern so children know what to expect, but the components should vary from day to day. For example, you might start with your theme song, the same one every day. This notifies children that circle time is about to start and that exciting times are in store. Follow this with a varying movement experience that involves children's bodies. Then, perhaps conduct some short community-building or shared writing activity that engages children's brains and is related to their current interests. Finally, end your circle time with a fun transition activity that varies daily.

Active circle times will be more interesting to children, more peaceful, and more fun for everyone. And fun should always be a major element in the early childhood classroom. Children who are having fun are less likely to exhibit challenging behaviors and are more likely to be learning.

Active vs. Passive Calendar Learning

Every morning starts the same in Ms. Latisha's classroom. During circle time, she points to the colorful calendar on the wall. "Who remembers what day it is?" she asks the gathered preK children. Children begin to shout out names of days until a child randomly hits on the correct one. The guessing game continues as the teacher asks about which day was yesterday and which day will come tomorrow. Despite having repeated this routine every morning of their preschool and preK years, children still do not grasp the ideas their teachers are trying to convey through the calendar activity.

Does the above scenario sound familiar? Teachers have the best of intentions in leading this experience every morning. Many lead calendar learning during

Figure 2.4 HOMES Ideas for Active Circle Times

H = Hands-on. Provide children with real materials to touch, experience, and manipulate during your circle times. When their hands are occupied, they are less likely to use them to mess with a child sitting nearby.

- When investigating trees, bring in branches, leaves, nuts, and roots for children to explore while talking.

- If the class is studying liquids, place small drops of various liquids on children's hands (be aware of allergies and health guidelines) so they can experience their properties.

- While discussing animals, bring in materials from or made by animals (such as a fur pelt, shark tooth, turtle shell, bird's nest, or other animal item you may have access to) that children can explore while making a chart about where animals live.

All of these materials can keep children's hands and brains engaged so they are more likely to attend to circle time.

O = Open-ended. Plan experiences or conversations that do not have preset answers or only one way of doing things.

- Open-ended conversations are those that start with a question or prompt that children can answer in many ways. Questions such as, "Where do you think rain comes from?" or, "What do you think birds do when it rains?" will lead to much richer discussions about weather than will, "Look outside and tell us the weather today." Likewise, asking, "What kind of house would you build if you lived under the ocean?" can lead children into a much deeper discussion on ocean life than will asking, "Where does a fish live?"

- Open-ended experiences are those that might lead in many different directions. For example,

"I found this box. Let's make a list of all the things it could be. Then let's pick one to make in the pretend center." Or write: "I woke up and was as small as an ant" on a piece of chart paper and invite children to finish the story.

Along with providing rich learning opportunities, these open-ended experiences allow children to play an active role in shaping what happens.

M = Meaningful. Build your circle times around topics that are of interest to children. Children will be much more engaged if you plan an experience around the latest movie they're talking about, for example, instead of discussing shamrocks because it is March.

E = Engaging. Give children opportunities to use both their minds and bodies during circle times. Plan experiences that allow children to move instead of requiring them to sit for the entire period. For example, say: "As we read this story, every time I read the word bear, let's stand up and roar" or, "When I say go, everyone go find something blue and bring it back to our circle."

Ask interesting questions that engage and challenge children's minds. Any of the following prompts encourage active thought.

- What do you think?

- How are they the same? How are they different?

- What might happen next?

- How did that happen?

- What might they be thinking?

- How do you feel about that?

- What would you do?

S = Sensory-oriented. Incorporate materials that engage children's senses. Introduce interesting items they can smell, hear, look at, taste, or feel. See the chart on page 58 for some ideas.

circle time without really thinking about it. It is just something that has always been done. They believe that through this repetition, children will come to understand time and number concepts. However, when viewed through the active learning lens, it becomes evident that this staple of the early childhood classroom is not really an effective teaching tool. On the HOMES scale, it scores a solid 0.

Figure 2.5 HOMES Active Learning Scale: Sample Circle Times

Circle Time A

Ms. Courtney puts out carpet squares and calls her preschoolers over for circle time. Most come over, but it takes her 5 to 7 minutes to gather the stragglers. Many children are excitedly talking about the garbage truck that came to empty the dumpster at the center, and it takes another 5 minutes to get the children to sit on their carpet squares. She repeats "1, 2, 3, eyes on me" until everyone is sitting quietly. She starts circle time with a "good morning" song, and children wave back as she welcomes them each by name. Next, she spends 5 minutes going over the calendar. As usual, Emily and Lyle name the days correctly as the other children contribute random days. Next, she picks Elijah as today's "weather helper." But before he can report back on what he saw through the window, Olivia interjects, "It is raining. I know because my blanket got all wet when my mom dropped it when we got out of the car." Elijah screams and runs to the corner of the room, very upset that Olivia ruined his chance to announce what he had seen. While Ms. Courtney tries to calm him down, two other children leave the circle to stand at the window to see if they can still see the garbage truck. It takes a good 5 minutes before Ms. Courtney can get the children refocused on circle time.

She reminds children that this week they are talking about animals. She posts some stock pictures of baby animals on a piece of chart paper. She makes a sound and asks children to identify the animal that makes that sound. When they get it correct, she circles the animal picture, asks children to identify the animal again, and writes the name of the animal under each picture. After a few turns, Pete starts sliding off his carpet square and stretches his feet to kick other children in the circle. Ms. Courtney pauses and says, "We will just wait until Pete is ready." The other children sit and wait for about 3 minutes while Pete giggles and continues to squirm. Finally, Ms. Courtney moves Pete to sit next to her. She continues the activity until all 10 animals are circled and named.

After the activity, one-by-one, she asks children to stand, spell their names, and announce which centers they are going to play in during free choice time. Anna throws herself on the floor and begins to cry, saying between sobs, "I wanted to go first." The teacher tells her that when she is quiet, she can have a turn. She calms down and, between sniffles, announces her choice.

After 35 minutes, Ms. Courtney is able to put away the carpet squares and get her materials ready for small groups. Let's look at this circle time through the lens of active learning.

Hands-on	Open-ended	Meaningful	Engaging	Sensory-oriented
There are no materials for children to explore, manipulate, or use during this circle time. Children's hands are idle for the entire time.	Ms. Courtney asks children to answer questions with one-word correct answers. Children have no opportunities to offer input or to drive the direction of the conversations or the experiences.	The activities are either routines that are done every day or are planned based on a predetermined theme. There is no attempt to connect the experiences to children's current interests.	The questions do not require children to think. Instead, children are only giving fact-based answers that many of them already know. No critical thinking, creativity, or problem-solving is involved. Children are also required to sit passively for the entire circle time, with no bodily engagement.	There is nothing very interesting for children to see, hear, smell, feel, or taste. The only thing they hear is the teacher's voice, and the only things to see are the stock pictures she posts on the paper.
0 points	0 points	0 points	0 points	0 points

Total Score: This circle time scores 0 points on the HOMES scale. Ms. Courtney's goal is to make sure children learn what they need for preK. However, as indicated by the children's behaviors, many of them are not interested and are learning very little during this time of the day.

Figure 2.5 HOMES Active Learning Scale: Sample Circle Times (continued)

Circle Time B

Mr. Charlie joins his preschoolers by the window as they excitedly watch the garbage truck empty the dumpster while it rains. He says, "It must be Wednesday, the garbage truck is here." And he talks with them about what they see. They discuss what it must be like to be a garbage collector and work in the rain. After, he announces to the class, "It is time for circle time. Remember the sound the garbage truck made when it moved in reverse? Let's all walk backward to the circle and make that sound." Most children join Mr. Charlie in the circle as he starts with the same song he sings every day. The children eagerly stretch, bend, shake, and join in with the lyrics before settling into comfortable positions on the carpet. While leading the song, Mr. Charlie scans the classroom to make sure Javi and Sarah, who did not come to circle time, are engaged in other activities.

Mr. Charlie uses masking tape to make two large intersecting circles on the carpet. While he works, he engages children in conversation and asks them to guess what he is doing. He asks children to name one way that people fasten two sides of a piece of clothing together, and Savannah eagerly says, "buttons." Mr. Charlie writes the word *button* on a piece of paper and puts it in one circle. He then asks for a pattern people sometimes have on their clothing. From the other side of the room, Javi responds, "stripes." As Javi answers, he moves closer to the group, interested in the activity the teacher is leading. Mr. Charlie writes *stripes* on a piece of paper and puts it in the other circle. He labels the area where the circles intersect with a premade sign that says *both* and the area outside the circle with one that reads *neither*.

He tells children that they are going to sort themselves into the appropriate spaces on the Venn diagram. So, if they have buttons, they stand in one circle. If they have stripes, they stand in the other circle. If they have both, they stand in the middle. And if they have neither, they stand outside both circles. He guides children as they eagerly figure out where they should stand. When they are all sorted, they count to see how many people are in each section. When the activity is done, Mr. Charlie takes a picture of the group and says that during small-group time, interested children can help him create a learning story that shows how they sorted themselves at circle time.

After this 15-minute circle time, the teacher transitions children to free choice time. He sings, "If your shirt is blue, hop to the center of your choice." He changes colors and movements until all children are involved in center activities.

Hands-on	Open-ended	Meaningful	Engaging	Sensory-oriented
Children are learning concepts by moving themselves to various locations. While they are not holding an item in their hands, they are using real objects (their clothes) to learn.	Mr. Charlie knows that he wants to lead a sorting activity with children and that he wants to involve clothing. But he involves children in determining the details of the experience.	Mr. Charlie starts by incorporating something of interest to children at that moment: the garbage truck. He incorporates their interest into the transition to circle time. He also uses children's own clothing in the sorting activity, which makes it a meaningful activity.	Children come to circle by walking backward like the garbage truck. They then sing a song incorporating a lot of movements. Children become scientists as they observe the attributes of their clothing, compare and contrast them, and make a decision about where to place themselves on the diagram. They also engage their bodies while moving to the appropriate section. Additionally, children move in interesting ways while transitioning to and from circle time.	This particular activity does not have a lot of sensory engagement, but children are being asked to see their clothes in perhaps a new way and to sing and make the sound of a truck backing up.
1 point	1 point	1 point	1 point	½ point

Total Score: Mr. Charlie's circle time scores 4.5 points on the HOMES scale. He makes sure children are actively involved in the experiences so that they are more likely to learn and will engage in fewer challenging behaviors.

Moreover, research shows that children are not ready to make sense of time concepts and the passage of time until they are between seven and ten years old.[15] Before that age, they struggle with calendar time because their brains are not ready to conceptualize the calendar and associated concepts. Time spent with children in a large group is limited and precious. Teachers should not waste it on practices that are neither effective nor appropriate.

This does not mean that you should not talk about days, dates, and time concepts with young children. In conversations with them, talk about today, yesterday, and tomorrow. Date any shared writing and art and point out that date to children. When they are developmentally ready to understand the calendar and related time concepts, the foundation you help them build now will make it that much easier.

Ms. Courtney and Mr. Charlie (in figure 2.5) both want what is best for their children, and they want them to have the tools they need to be successful learners. Probably on paper, both of their circle times are an appropriate fifteen minutes long. But, because Ms. Courtney's circle time is passive, it is punctuated by challenging behaviors that drag the experience out to a developmentally inappropriate thirty-five minutes. A circle time that varies in content each day, incorporates fun, and reflects what we know about how children learn will make this time of day less of a chore and more of a community-building experience that everyone looks forward to.

Chapter Summary

The successful gardener knows that while individual plants vary, most of them need water, soil, and sun to grow. For young children, active learning is the equivalent of these basic needs. When teachers incorporate these concepts into the activities they facilitate and the environments they create, they are providing children with the nutrients they need to be successful. Classrooms designed to teach in the way children learn, instead of asking children to learn the way we want to teach, are those where deeper learning happens and fewer challenging behaviors occur.

Chapter 3

Building Relationships with Children:
Get to Know Your Buds

A diligent gardener learns all she can about the nature and needs of each plant species in her garden. At the same time, she also must understand the individual needs of each seedling so that it can grow and bear fruit to its full potential. Likewise, an early childhood educator must have a commanding knowledge of young children's development, as well as knowing about the individual development, needs, and interests of each child in her care.

Along with building a foundation on the elements of active learning discussed in chapter 2, forging strong relationships with children is the most important step you can take to reduce incidents of challenging behavior in your classroom. When you know your children well, you can create environments that are responsive to their needs. When you understand children's developmental needs, you can design learning experiences that fall in their zones of proximal development so that children are appropriately challenged as opposed to bored or frustrated. And when you understand their social-emotional needs, you can anticipate problems and respond appropriately to issues that arise. Building strong relationships with individual children leads to a strong classroom community in which challenging behaviors are less likely to occur. There are many strategies you can use to foster relationships with the children in your care.

Call Children by Their Names

"What's in a name?" Shakespeare wrote, "That which we call a rose by any other name would smell as sweet." While this may be true, to children, there is no sound quite so sweet as the sound of their own name (unless, of course, it is their full name—then they know they are in trouble). Parents often put much thought and energy into finding the perfect name for an unborn child, poring over baby books and websites and trying out the sounds of names in the quest to find the right one. Usually, the name parents decide on is filled with meaning and importance for the family. Once bestowed on a child, the name becomes the most beautiful word of all to the child and her family.

By simply using children's names, those meaningful family words, in your classroom, you build relationships with children and their families. This means learning to say difficult names instead of finding and using nicknames that are easier to pronounce. You also honor children when you use their names instead of generic terms like *sweetie*, *kiddo*, and *honey*. Often, teachers see these as terms of endearment, but if they are used too frequently, they can serve to strip children of their individuality and label them as one of many who are all the same.

You also build relationships with children and families when you not only learn children's names, but also find out the significance of each child's name.

When I was a young teacher, I had a boy in my room who had a very rare name that was difficult for me to pronounce. His mother had given birth to him as a teenager, and I found myself judging her and the name she had "saddled" her child with (in my slanted opinion). Narrow-mindedly, I assumed that she had simply strung some syllables together in a way that was pleasing to her young ears.

Like many teachers, every week I highlighted a child in the class as the Star of the Week. Part of the information I gathered was the origin of the child's name, to celebrate where it had come from. When it was this boy's turn, I interviewed him and his mom so I could make his special poster. When I asked his mom about his name, her answer humbled me. "I was a young mother," she explained. "I knew that it would be hard and that I would probably be overwhelmed and feel lost sometimes. I never wanted to lose sight of what this child is. His name is an ancient word for *gift from God*. I always wanted to remember that my boy is a gift from God for which I should be thankful."

I don't know if the mother remembers our exchange, but this conversation changed how I viewed children's names and taught me how meaningful those names are to the parents who bestow them. I came to realize the importance of honoring each child's name, of showing that honor by learning to pronounce it correctly, and of using it frequently in my interactions with the child.

Along with learning and using children's names yourself, you build relationships with children by helping them learn and value each other's names. This is especially important at the start of a school year or when new children transition into the classroom. Singing songs, leading fingerplays, and playing games that incorporate children's names are fun and engaging ways to celebrate each individual. (*Note*: having each child stand up during group time to spell his or her name is not.)

Plan for Individual Interactions

It is difficult for children to be a member of a large group for so many hours a day and to share the attention of adults all the time. While large groups cannot be avoided in many group-learning situations, that does not mean children must be deprived of individual attention. Just as you plan large-group times, small-group times, and fun, large-motor experiences for the playground, you can also plan for individual interactions. It's often easy to find opportunities to interact individually with those children who are social leaders, who seek out teachers and are friendly and outgoing. There are also plenty of opportunities to share individual moments with those children who might challenge teachers. After an episode of challenging behavior, teachers often spend time with the child, providing correction or comfort. You might also look for ways to affirm these children and attempt to build them up despite their behavior challenges. However, it's often more difficult to share individual interactions with those children who are on neither side of the continuum, those who blend in and generally go with the flow. They can be easy to pass over in the hubbub of classroom activity. And yet, it is with these children that teachers need to intentionally build relationships.

While it may at first seem oddly formal, some teachers find it helpful to have a tracking system for individual interactions with children. You might keep a tracking sheet under other papers on a clipboard. As you reflect on your day, you can add a dot next to each child's name with whom you had a one-on-one interaction. As the week goes on, you can intentionally seek out those children who do not yet have any dots.

Strong relationships are formed as you get to know and appreciate children as individuals. This bond happens as you engage children in conversations, play with individual children, and, even if just for a couple of minutes, make each child feel like the most important person in the classroom.

Take Advantage of Stolen Moments

Along with your primary job of caring for and educating children, many other tasks are required in the classroom, as you well know. There always seems to be another piece of paperwork to complete, another area of the classroom to clean, or some other task to finish before the day is over. Because of these demands, you might logically take advantage of slow times to do these odd jobs. Slow times may include naptime, when most children are asleep, or the start or end of the day, when only a few children are around. Sometimes, as you get involved in this work, children may be, understandably, regulated to areas of the classroom or activities that serve to keep them out of the way. This might mean sitting on a carpet with a book at the end of the day as you fill out paperwork or clean up. Unfortunately, teachers often report that challenging behaviors are especially prevalent during these times of day.

As tempting as it is to complete your odd jobs during these times, they are perfect opportunities to share moments with individual children. Sit and read a story with the first two children in the classroom. Rub a child's back as she lies awake on her cot during naptime. Enlist the last few children as partners in the cleanup process at the end of the day, engaging them in conversations throughout. These stolen moments help build relationships with children. When children feel involved and important, they are less likely to engage in problematic behaviors.

A childcare center director once told me about her experience with a toddler named Kellie. Kellie was prone to tantrums and seemed to have trouble getting used to the center. She was also the first child to arrive every morning. The teacher had a few tasks to do in the morning, so the director would take charge of Kellie for the first few minutes. She would take Kellie into her office, sit her in a chair with some dry cereal, and go about the many duties that awaited her. She sometimes chatted with Kellie while she worked and always responded to Kellie's attempts to interact, but her focus was on her work. Kellie waited around until the teacher came in, and after a quick hug, the director would send her on her way.

The director recounted how one morning, instead of going into her office, she took Kellie into the infant room. She sat in a rocking chair, held Kellie in her lap, and rocked her while gently singing. She and Kellie both relaxed as the toddler's body melted into her arms. Instantly, the director knew this would become their ritual. They would spend these first few minutes of the day in the rocking chair until the teacher was ready to open the classroom and welcome Kellie and the other children who would soon arrive. The director explained that not only did she and Kellie look forward to these stolen moments, but Kellie's tantrums lessened as this interaction became a daily habit. By making Kellie the focus of her attention for those few minutes, the director eased the girl's transition into the center and let her know that she was a valued member of the community.

Making children the center of attention for a couple of minutes as opportunities present themselves is a small investment of time and energy that will pay off in dividends of happier, calmer, and better adjusted children. When taken advantage of, stolen moments can be a special gift for both teacher and child.

Understand Children's Preferences

Children are unique and have unique preferences. Eighteen-month-old Noah might resist having his diaper changed unless he is holding his favorite toy.

Maybe Emma is the social butterfly in the preK classroom, but she might need five minutes by herself in the cozy corner with her blanket before transitioning into the classroom every morning. Baby Bennet might only be comforted with his pacifier and a gentle rubbing of the back of his head. Samiya loves stories, but she may be better able to concentrate when she walks around while listening versus sitting still. As teachers spend time with children, they come to know and appreciate children's unique tendencies and dispositions. Instead of trying to dissuade children of these preferences, teachers build strong relationships when they honor each child's special way of interacting with the world.

Teachers also help build strong relationships when they make sure all caregivers are in the loop about a child's preferences. Every teacher who may spend time with Molly, for example, should know that she goes right to sleep if a teacher gently rubs her chest for a couple of minutes. Even a substitute teacher needs to be aware that Simon needs a few minutes on his cot after naptime before he can get up and participate in the rest of the day or that Sophie sometimes is tired because her big brother is deployed and she loves to talk with him whenever he can call, even if it is in the middle of the night. When all teachers know and respond to a child's preferences, he is more likely to feel that he is in a safe place where the big people know him and are ready to take care of him. This feeling of security leads to a child being much better prepared to navigate the social and behavioral expectations of an early childhood classroom.

Incorporate Children's Interests

Imagine that you are invited to a party. When you arrive, the hostess gleefully points out everything she has arranged for her guests. Your friend is a vegan, fantasy-novel-loving, karaoke-singing, red wine aficionado, and the party reflects all her favorites. Unfortunately, you are not a fan of any of these things, and neither are most of the other guests. As you look around, you get the sense that the hostess only took into consideration her own tastes as she planned the party and that your and the other guests' experiences do not hold much importance for her.

Now imagine another party. As you walk through the door, the host greets you with delight and directs you toward a table in the corner. "I remember you saying how much you prefer sparkling water," he says. "I have three different flavors right here. Let me know which is your favorite." As each guest enters, your friend points out something at the party that reflects that guest's tastes and interests.

You might have fun at both parties, but you probably leave the second one feeling much more understood and cherished. Strong relationships result when teachers cultivate this sense of individual importance in every child. You can do this by understanding what children like and sprinkling the classroom and your discussions with reflections of those interests. Children's interests can be held front and center as teachers plan classroom experiences and enhancements. Nothing says "I know and like you" like making sure each child finds something in the classroom that was put there just for her. For example:

"Adie, I heard you talking about the monster trucks you saw with your uncle. There are some big wheels on the playground that we can explore when we go outside."

"You sure liked the movie about penguins, Nico. I found this magazine with lots of pictures of penguins and thought you might like it. I also have a special story about penguins for literacy circle today."

"That is so cool that your grandma is visiting all the way from China, Lin. Your mom sent in some cookbooks and food boxes from your house, so we can put them in the pretend center."

When children see themselves and their interests reflected in the classroom, they come to trust that they are known and valued. That sense of being cared for is the foundation of a strong relationship.

Celebrate Accomplishments

There is a lot to learn and master when one is starting out in life. Talking, walking, eating with a fork, going potty on the toilet—it seems like every day brings a new expectation or task to undertake. Teachers build relationships with children and families as they find ways to celebrate these accomplishments. The classroom community can celebrate together when a baby takes those first steps (after it has been seen at home—see "How to Handle Milestones" below) or when a toddler masters the difficult task of putting on his own shoes. Not every milestone calls for a group celebration, but a celebratory note home to families lets children know that teachers are paying attention and that they think all those new things being learned are pretty cool.

HOW TO HANDLE MILESTONES

Infant teachers sometimes have the difficult task of noticing and celebrating a baby's developmental milestones while being conscious of the sense of loss families often feel about not being present to observe these exciting firsts. As part of building relationships with families, it is usually a good idea to let them be the ones to capture these accomplishments. For example, a baby might take her first tentative steps in the classroom. Instead of telling her dad at pickup, you might say something like, "She is so close to walking. I can tell it will happen any minute now. I bet you might see those first steps tonight or tomorrow!" This message lets family members know that teachers are watching and happily anticipating the moment without taking the moment away from the family. Each center may have a different approach to this dilemma. It is important to have the conversation as a center so that everyone is on the same page.

Acknowledge Strengths

All humans, including children, appreciate hearing when they are good at something. It feels good to be viewed as competent and to know that someone notices your proficiency. Sometimes, teachers are more apt to notice where children are weak and will focus on those areas where they need to support children's learning and development. While this is natural, it is important to keep in mind and acknowledge children's strengths. You can celebrate children's strengths by acknowledging them to the child, referring children to each other for help, and sharing their accomplishments with families.

Teachers build relationships and children's sense of self-efficacy when they acknowledge children's strengths as immediately as possible using descriptive language. For example:

"Thanks for putting the tops on all the markers, Caleb. The art center always looks so good when you clean it."

"I saw you helping Makayla up after she fell. You are a good friend, Sam."

"You made it so fast from there to here, Olive! You are a really fast runner."

When teachers deliver statements like these, they indicate to children that they notice children's strengths and value their contributions to the classroom community.

Referring children to each other for help builds children's sense of their own abilities and develops a classroom community in which children value and appreciate each other. For example, you might notice a child struggling to work the tape dispenser. Instead of stepping in to help, you might say, "You should see if Henry can help you. He is a pro at getting tape out of this thing." Or, you might notice a child trying to use a jump rope. You might say to another child, "Frankie, you are doing so well jumping rope. Maybe you can go help Jazmine. It looks like she could use a hand." In these situations, a teacher facilitates children learning from each other while celebrating the individual strengths children bring to the classroom.

Teachers are often quick to write notes to families when children need something for the classroom or when they exhibit challenging behaviors. Likewise, teachers can use the power of the written word to share what children do well, ideally on a regular basis, such as once a month. Nothing will brighten families' days like reading a note that lets them know they are not the only ones who see their child as special and value their child's unique gifts. Emailed pictures or notes are sure to bring a smile to the middle of a family member's workday. And, if the budget allows, these notes will have an even greater impact if they are mailed to a child's home. Positive words, in verbal and written form, go a long way in building strong relationships with children and families. See chapter 7 for more on creating family partnerships.

Respect a Child's Rights

Positive relationships are fostered in an atmosphere of mutual respect. At its most basic, *respect* means accepting the fact that another person has certain rights and privileges. Teachers build an environment of respect as they show children, through their behavior and words, their belief that all children have unalienable rights as members of the classroom community. These rights are as follows:

The right to be heard. You show respect for this right when you indicate that you are truly listening to children. This means getting down on their level, making eye contact while they are talking, and responding in ways that show you have heard them.

The right to be safe. This right encompasses both a child's physical and psychological safety. Physically, this means that you create environments that are free of hazards, you treat children gently, you guide children in navigating the world, and you stop harmful behaviors as soon as possible. Psychologically, this means that you do not diminish, bully, or insult children (nor do you allow other children to demonstrate these behaviors); you refrain from asking children to complete a task or behave in a way that is well beyond their years or abilities; and you regard and honor children's feelings.

A CHILD'S BILL OF RIGHTS

The Right to Be Heard

The Right to Be Safe

The Right to Kindness

The Right to Be a Child and an Individual

The right to kindness. You show respect for this right when you are gentle with children's bodies, souls, and minds. Kindness comes through as you hold babies and talk with them as you feed them, instead of leaving them propped on a pillow on the floor or in a bouncy seat. Children feel kindness as you rub their backs to help them calm down for naptime. You show kindness as you give toddlers notice that you are going to change their diapers instead of snatching them out of play without warning. You show kindness as you enthusiastically greet school-age kids with high fives and hugs instead of giving them instructions as soon as they walk into the room. Kind classrooms are those in which smiles, laughter, and a genuine sense of appreciation for children prevail.

The right to be a child and an individual. You show respect for the right to be a child by creating classroom environments and experiences that are developmentally appropriate. You do not place social or behavioral expectations on children that are beyond their abilities. And you value each stage of development and plan accordingly instead of trying to rush children into the next stage.

You show respect for the right to be an individual by considering the needs and interests of each child. You get to know children as individuals and take joy in each child instead of trying to shape him into someone else. Children feel this respect when they trust that you have their best interests in mind and that you know and love them. You give this message of respect by saying to each child (through words and behaviors), "Wow, you really are a cool kid. I'm glad you are you. And I'm glad you are here."

These four rights are the behavioral indicators of a classroom built around respect. Along with guiding a teacher's attitudes and actions, these rights can serve as the foundation for classroom rules about how children interact with the materials and each other. You can help children understand that they are not and will not be friends with everyone in the classroom. This is not a realistic expectation. However, friend or not, every person is worthy of respect.

Does Someone Adore My Baby?

There is an activity I facilitate when I lead training sessions with teachers and families. I ask them to close their eyes and imagine the face of a child they hold dear personally (for teachers, this means a child they know outside of their professional roles). I then ask them to imagine that they are dropping off that child with a group of strangers for eight to ten hours. And I ask, "What do you want for that child?" The answers vary, but almost always the first two mentioned are "love" and "safety." One time, I was leading this activity in Atlanta, and I had already moved on to the next part of the activity when a teacher spoke up from the back of the room. "Wait, wait," she interjected, "Love isn't what I want for my child. That isn't strong enough. I need to feel like those people who have my baby adore her."

Adore is a powerful word. It goes above and beyond *love* and suggests that a child is at the center of someone's universe. Each child deserves to feel adored at some point during her day, and families need to feel like the person they leave their child with has eyes for only her, at least some of the time.

While in the classroom it is impossible to give children the same level of attention they would receive in a one-on-one care situation, it is not impossible to make each child feel adored for a few minutes each day. For those few minutes, the child can feel like his teacher's attention is his alone.

Chapter Summary

By putting in place all the components outlined in this chapter, you are nurturing strong relationships with the children in your care. Cultivating these relationships along with building responsive and appropriate learning environments are sun and rain to the early childhood classroom. When children can bask in the sun of the teacher's attention and be nurtured in a fertile space that provides them with the cognitive and emotional supports they need, they will grow healthy and hearty. Challenging behaviors are far less likely to occur when teachers know and value children as individuals and build classrooms that reflect these best practices.

Chapter 4

Teaching Social Skills:
Support the Plants in Your Care

When a teacher designs classroom environments around children's developmental and learning needs, plans learning experiences based on active learning, and builds strong relationships with children, he is like the gardener who carefully prepares the ground to enable his plants to thrive. However, even with exceptional soil and growing conditions, a seedling might, at times, need special attention to help it along if it struggles and veers slightly off path. In the same way, there are times when a child may struggle and exhibit puzzling behaviors because he has not yet learned an alternative behavior in response to a social situation.

Young children are emotionally immature and do not yet have the skills to navigate the myriad social situations they encounter every day in the early childhood classroom. Sharing is hard, watching out for others seems unfair, waiting is boring, and taking turns is exasperating. Many teachers go into early childhood classrooms prepared to teach colors, shapes, and letters. Yet sometimes they forget that an important part of the early educator's role is to teach the skills children need to be part of a classroom community. In many cases, the behaviors a teacher may view as challenging are instead an unintended result of a child not yet knowing how to control her emotions and impulses or not yet competent in social skills. Child development expert Dan Gartrell calls these behaviors *mistaken* instead of challenging.

An example of a mistaken behavior is when a child runs toward the door after the teacher announces that it is time to go outside. While running, he accidently knocks over another child in his path in his excitement to reach the door. This was not an intentional act. The boy did not mean to push the other child. He was just so thrilled to be going outside, and that feeling got the better of him. It is up to the teacher to help him learn to manage those impulses and emotions and stay aware and respectful of the other children around him.

Children come into early childhood settings from a variety of backgrounds and with wide ranges of knowledge. Some children know how to hold a crayon; others have never experienced one. Some hear stories every night; some fall asleep watching TV. In the same way, children come into classrooms with a wide variety of social experiences and understandings. Children are not born knowing that hitting others is wrong. Over time, some have actually found that hitting can be very effective. If you have a truck I want and I hit you, there is a good chance I will get the truck . . . at least until I learn that you hit harder or an adult intervenes to take the truck away from me. Again, it is the teacher's role to help a child learn more effective ways to traverse the many social challenges that come from being a member of a group for eight to ten hours a day.

In these social situations, how a teacher responds can either serve to punish or to teach. Responses that punish may make a child feel bad about her behavior (even though it may have been an accident) and might stop the behavior temporarily. These responses, however, do not teach children an alternate behavior that is socially acceptable and more effective. Just as the gardener does not punish a plant for failing to bloom, a teacher does not discipline a child for mistaken behaviors—instead recognizing that these behaviors provide an opportunity to teach and guide the child's behavioral responses. As teachers move away from those responses that punish and become more adept at using those that teach, they will find that the classroom becomes a more nurturing environment in which more children find their way to bloom.

Less Effective Responses to Challenging Behavior

In this section, we will look at some common responses to behavior that do not effectively teach social skills. Then, in the following section, we will also look at responses to behaviors that address mistakes *and* serve to teach children helpful alternate behaviors.

Punishments

The definition of a punishment is an action taken in retribution for an offense. It is about penalizing a child for a perceived slight or misbehavior. Punishment is sometimes harsh and can involve yelling or belittling. Punishment can also include returning a child's behavior. For example, grabbing a toy back from a child so he knows how it feels. Punishment is sometimes administered from a state of anger and is enacted without explanation or an attempt to help the child understand what he did wrong or what he can do the next time he is faced with the same situation.

In a childcare or classroom setting, punishment might include spanking (which, sadly, is still legal in schools in some states), raising one's voice at a child, or abruptly removing a child from a situation. While these responses are viewed as inappropriate discipline by most state licensing agencies, they still occur in many centers, both licensed and unlicensed. At times, these actions arise out of frustration. At other times, they occur because adults truly believe children will change their behavior as a result of the punishment. The truth is that punishment may stop a behavior temporarily, but it does not teach a child the expected behavior. Furthermore, instead of building a trusting relationship with the adults in a classroom, a child may learn to fear them. Instead of making good choices from a place of understanding social norms, children may seek to avoid punishment by lying, hiding mistakes, or being afraid to make any choices for fear of angering an adult. Worse, studies have found that corporal punishment in childhood negatively affects children's cognitive ability and how they perform in school. And while spanking a child can sometimes lead to short-term compliance, it also is associated with many harmful social and emotional outcomes, such as increased aggression, internalized feelings of inadequacy, and mental health challenges. With so many other possible options for guiding a child's behavior, there is never an excuse for using physical punishment or coercion in the early childhood classroom.

Behavior Charts

If behavior charts were effective in changing children's behaviors, a teacher would not need them in the classroom after a month. If they worked, after that month, children would have learned all the skills they need to be in the classroom community and would use them consistently. Instead, usually the same children find their names in the red zone, or have their apples removed from the tree, or watch their names get written on the board, or whatever other form a behavior chart might take in any given classroom. In most cases, the children who are, from the start, more able to understand and follow social expectations get additional praise for their behavior. Those who are not do not learn what they need to change nor how to do it. They are just repeatedly reminded of their social failings, which often causes them grief and leads to even more challenging behaviors.

A behavior chart doesn't teach children classroom expectations or how to meet them. It only keeps track of their successes and failures in meeting those expectations. And it keeps track in a very public, and often humiliating, manner—both for the child and the child's family members. Everyone in the classroom or center knows which children failed to meet expectations. Imagine coming to work to find a list of staff names posted in the lobby. As you go about your day, the director observes your actions and reflects these observations by adding green, yellow, or red clothespins next to your name on the list. By the end of the day, all your colleagues and the children, their families, and random visitors would know if you had met the director's expectations or not. Yet, you probably wouldn't even know what you had done to fail or to succeed. And if you had failed, you surely would not have received guidance on alternatives to help you succeed.

As in the case of the imaginary staff chart, some children in a typical early childhood classroom would be devastated to have their behavior broadcast to the rest of the world. As with punishments, behavior charts may cause children to become afraid of trying anything new for fear of making a mistake that results in their names being "turned to red." They may remain "on green" perpetually, not because they have learned social norms, but because they dare not try anything new. On the opposite end of the spectrum are those children who do not care what color is assigned to their names. They will go about their daily lives indifferent to the chart. It has no impact on their behavior and no impact on their understanding of social expectations. When a teacher threatens to "turn their names to red," these children may simply shrug and continue on the same behavioral path.

Using a behavior chart to manage behavior is like trying to teach a sport without providing a clear understanding of its rules, instead simply adding or removing points as the players fumble around trying to understand the game. Children often have no idea why their names are moved from one area of the chart to another, especially if their status changes throughout the day. Instead of learning social expectations, children may feel that the chart solely reflects the whims of the teacher.

> Nicole, a coworker of mine, tells the story of when she picked up her daughter from kindergarten a couple of weeks into the new school year. She asked her daughter how everything was going at school. "Great," her daughter responded. "Mommy, I am so good at being on yellow," she reported enthusiastically. Nicole already knew that behavior charts are ineffective in molding children's behaviors. Yet, she told me, it was not until this moment that she fully realized how little her daughter understood the chart and, thus, how truly inane it was as a form of behavior modification. Her daughter was thrilled that she had mastered the skill of staying in the yellow range—the warning range—of the behavior chart.

Time-Outs

Contrary to popular belief, when children are sent to time-out, they are not spending the time thinking about what they have done wrong. Instead, they may be thinking about how unfair the teacher is, how they can get out of where they are, what they ate for lunch earlier, and anything else besides what they might do differently in a similar situation next time.

Time-outs came to popularity as a piece of the parenting arsenal in the late 1950s. While they were first introduced to parents as an alternative to spanking, they quickly became a common behavior modification technique in the early childhood arena, to the extent that many classrooms have a permanent time-out corner, carpet, or chair. Sending a child to time-out is often the go-to response to challenging behaviors in the preschool classroom.

However, rather than being a teaching tool, time-outs are a punishment. They serve to isolate and humiliate struggling children instead of providing them with the tools they need to be successful in the classroom. Children in time-out are more focused on their feelings of despair or anger at being punished than on learning social skills. And children cannot learn the social skills they need when they are separated from the group. As education pioneer John Dewey taught, the only way to teach social skills is to be in a social situation. To try to do otherwise is to try to teach a child to swim without the benefit of water.

At times, a child might need time away from the group in order to calm down. In those cases, a teacher should remain close to the child, help him work his way through his feelings, and provide him with the skills necessary to return to the group when he is ready. Some classrooms have spaces where children can go to calm down or just have quiet time away from others. Children can use these spaces freely, and if needed, an adult can be there to support a child who is struggling. A child who feels connected and supported is better able to learn the social skills needed to be part of the classroom community.

Unclear Requests

In the quest to use positive language with children, sometimes teachers end up describing behaviors using unclear phrasing. Instead of teaching social norms, these phrases can add to children's confusion about what is expected of them. **Figure 4.1** on pages 82–84 looks at some common phrases teachers use and how those phrases can be reframed to clearly and directly communicate expectations to children while still using positive language whenever possible.

NO, THANK YOU . . . FOR WHAT?

I was once observing in a preK classroom in Michigan. Usually when I observe, I tuck myself in a corner and try to be as unobtrusive as possible. As I watched a circle time, a young boy came into the classroom. He was finishing up his breakfast, so the teacher directed him to sit at a table near me until he was done. The boy noticed me, and we struck up a conversation about who I was, why I was there, and what I was writing on my paper. From the carpet where she was leading the group activity, the teacher called across the room, "No, thank you, Marquis." The little boy, startled and confused, looked at me for guidance as to why he was in trouble. I subtly shrugged my shoulders. Both of us, with no idea why we had been admonished, went back to our tasks of eating and observing. If I, as a grown adult, had no idea what Marquis was doing wrong, you can bet that he did not have the social understanding to figure it out.

When later reflecting on the interaction, I realized that the teacher was probably attempting to support me in my work by redirecting Marquis's attention away from what I was doing. While I appreciated this, using clear and direct language, such as, "Marquis, please finish eating and join us," would have provided him better instruction for how to meet the classroom expectations.

Teachers may also create ambiguity when they state expectations as questions, as discussed in chapter 1. For example, "Are you ready to lie on your cot?" gives the impression to a child that she can respond, "No, I'm not ready. I want to play more." Likewise, "I'm going to wipe your nose, okay?" presents a child with the opportunity to say, "No, I don't want my nose wiped." If there is not a choice, do not give children one. Instead, state firmly and clearly what you expect: "It is naptime. Come get on your cot." "You have some yuck on your face. I'm going to wipe your nose now." These phrases provide children with a clear understanding of your expectations. If children are to understand social skills, teachers must be direct in helping them understand the expectations and giving them the skills they need to be successful.

Figure 4.1 Clarifying Common Phrases Used by Teachers

WHAT TEACHERS SAY	WHAT TEACHERS MEAN	WHY THE PHRASE IS CONFUSING	WHAT TO SAY INSTEAD
"Nice hands."	This command may be used to mean any number of things. Teachers may use it to request that a child stop hurting another child or stop using her hands for anything a teacher does not find acceptable.	In some ways, this phrase removes responsibility from the child. "It is my hands that are causing the problem. *They* are not being nice." Unless teachers follow up the phrase with clarification about what the child's hands are doing that isn't nice, the child may not understand the teacher's expectation at all. Because of the teacher's intervention, a child may stop whatever she was doing but without understanding what she was doing that drew the teacher's response and what she should do instead.	Say something like, "Hands off," "Hands down," or, "Please stop [behavior]" instead.
"No, thank you."	Teachers use this phrase in response to any number of behaviors. Generally, it is used to let children know that they are doing something that is not acceptable.	The phrase, while polite, provides no guidance for children as to what they are doing wrong and what they should do instead. The phrase can actually confuse children. We teach children to say "No, thank you" to be polite, especially in response to a person offering something nice that we can't accept at that moment. For example, when someone offers you a sandwich but you are not hungry. Usually, the behavior a child is demonstrating that elicits this response is not desirable at *any* time, so why would an adult say "No, thank you" in	Directly address the behavior that is unacceptable. If children are standing and you want them to sit, say, "Sit down, please." If they are playing with their food, say, "Eat your food." Unless teachers give children clear instructions and feedback on their behaviors, children cannot be expected to understand the behavioral expectations.

Figure 4.1 Clarifying Common Phrases Used by Teachers (continued)

WHAT TEACHERS SAY	WHAT TEACHERS MEAN	WHY THE PHRASE IS CONFUSING	WHAT TO SAY INSTEAD
"No, thank you." (continued)		response to it? For example, when a child is throwing food, why would we want to thank him for that behavior?	
"Hitting hurts."	This phrase and others like it are used in response to a child hitting or otherwise hurting another child. When saying this, a teacher is essentially telling a child not to hit another child.	This phrase offers information, but it does not offer direction. Usually, when a child hits another child, she is doing so to hurt him. Either the other child hurt her first, or the other child is doing something for which he deserves to be hurt (in the eyes of the hitter). So, telling the child that hitting hurts simply affirms information she already knows.	In these cases, a teacher can provide instruction with direct phrases such as, "Don't hit" or, "Hands down." A teacher can also redirect the child with a pillow (or other soft object) and instructions such as, "We don't hit people. You can squeeze this instead." Teachers can also acknowledge the feelings behind the child's actions, "You are very angry because he took your truck. I get it. But I can't let you hit. I will help you find another way to get the truck back."
"Use your words."	Teachers often use this phrase after the previous one, "Hitting hurts," to encourage children to express their feelings or needs through words as opposed to physical aggression.	First, this phrase does not tell children why they are being asked to use their words or how using their words would change the situation. Second, young children often do not have the words they need to defuse situations or clearly express themselves.	Instead of prompting children with this broad phrase, teachers can help children navigate a situation by giving them the actual words they need. "Ask her to please move" gives children the exact words they need as an alternative to pushing another child. "Tell him you're not done with the truck" provides instruction for how to respond when someone takes a toy. "Tell her not to hit you" guides a child in how to respond when hit. In many cases, if children knew the words to use in these social situations, they would. It is up to teachers to teach them so they can be more successful the next time.
"Catch a bubble."	This phrase means that children are to puff out their cheeks (as if holding a bubble in their mouths) and close their lips. Teachers often give this direction when they want children to be quiet.	Teachers think that this phrase makes a game out of being quiet. And in many ways it does. However, children may not understand that underneath the game is a real request—that they be quiet.	When teachers need children to be quiet, the most direct approach is to say, "Please be quiet so you can hear me" or, "Listen." With clear language, a teacher can convey to children exactly what she needs from them in that moment.

Figure 4.1 Clarifying Common Phrases Used by Teachers (continued)

WHAT TEACHERS SAY	WHAT TEACHERS MEAN	WHY THE PHRASE IS CONFUSING	WHAT TO SAY INSTEAD
"Make good choices."	This is a generic phrase that adults use to encourage children to behave in acceptable ways in a variety of situations.	When children display challenging behaviors, especially in social situations, these behaviors are rarely the result of a rational, well-thought-out choice. Their behavior is a form of communication. In this case, they are incapable of making good choices as they may not be in rational control of their behaviors. This phrase can also cause confusion about the definition of *good*. Some children may feel that the good choice is to run around the classroom because their bodies are telling them to run. Or, a good choice may be for the child to say something mean because his feelings were hurt. The word *good* is ambiguous and loaded with cultural context and understanding. Finally, the phrase assumes that whatever behavioral choice children are making now is not socially acceptable, but it does not specify what "wrong" choice they are making.	Try to be direct and specific with children. They will learn socially acceptable behaviors when teachers point out what they are doing that needs to stop and clearly provide them with an alternative behavior. For example, if a child is trying to throw the ball over the fence, a teacher might say, "If it goes over the fence, we lose the ball. You can throw it in the basket or give it to me." You are correcting the behavior and providing two very clear alternate "good" choices.

Ultimatums

The quickest way to get into a power struggle is to issue an ultimatum to a child. "We are not going outside until you pick up all the blocks" does not serve to teach a child social skills. Instead, it is more likely to make a child feel powerless. He may react to this feeling by digging in his heels and, before you know it, you are engaged in a power struggle.

Unfortunately, there are usually no winners in a power struggle. The child who refuses to pick up the blocks will feel like he loses if he gives in and picks up the blocks. The teacher feels like she loses if she gives in and lets the child get away with leaving a pile of blocks on the floor. Meanwhile, the other children look on, waiting and wondering what they did to deserve not being able to go outside and anxious to see who will come out of this stand-off the victor.

The easiest way to avoid a power struggle is not to issue ultimatums. Instead, use other strategies to help children learn social skills. Unfortunately, however, we often do not recognize an ultimatum-induced power struggle until we are in the middle of it. Once a teacher is in one, it is important to remove the winning-and-losing aspect from the equation and to find a graceful way to exit the situation. Remember, the goal is to teach children the skills they need, not to teach them a lesson or to win a battle of wills.

In the previous example with the blocks, to end the struggle the teacher might say, "So let's all pitch in and get the job done" or, "Do you want to hand me the blocks, or do you want me to hand them to you?" Either way, she has defused the situation and is teaching the children valuable social skills like helping others and pitching in to get a job done.

Requiring Apologies

How many times have we used the phrase, "Say you're sorry." While apologies are a wonderful way to express remorse for an unintended action or result, forced apologies do nothing to help children learn, and they can backfire if children come to believe that a quick "I'm sorry" can fix any situation. There may be times when a child sincerely wants to apologize, to try to atone for some mistake. But forcing children to apologize puts them in a situation where they may have to lie, especially if they are not truly sorry for whatever they did. Merely saying the words does nothing to help children understand why their action requires an apology. It also does not help them remedy the situation. And it does not provide them with guidance on alternate actions they might have taken instead.

The same can be true for making children hug and say they are friends after an altercation. All children do not have to be friends. They must be kind to each other and treat each other with respect, but they aren't all friends. Making children hug brushes over their emotions and does not give them the tools they need to work through social conflicts. It can also send mixed messages about children's autonomy over who can touch their bodies and when.

Expecting Empathy

Children are naturally egocentric. They have very little concern for the experience of others—not because they are mean, but because their brains have not yet developed the capacity for empathy. Often, teachers expect children to learn by considering the feelings of others. For example, they might say, "How do you think that makes him feel?" after one child takes a toy from another. The truth is that the young child often cannot learn from the experience of another, because she cannot imagine and has little concern for what another is going through. The important thing to that child is that now she has the toy.

Still, just because children don't yet have the capacity for empathy doesn't mean that teachers can't help them recognize and name others' feelings. Instead of "How do you think he feels?" a teacher can help a child develop that understanding by saying, "Look, he is crying and looks sad because you knocked him down. Let's help him up and see what we can do to make him feel better." By pointing out feelings, we help children develop empathy and recognize that their actions impact others. While we cannot expect empathy from young children, it is never too early to model it for them. With older children (age three and up), as we start to see the genesis of empathy and the understanding that others have unique feelings and experiences, we can start to provide them with words and actions to build relationships and be part of the classroom community.

Comparisons

There usually tend to be some children in the class who are very adept in social situations and who have a knack for following the rules. Teachers are often tempted to use these children as models to encourage other children to conform to classroom expectations. They might say, "I like the way Alice is sitting. Thank you, Alice. Can you all sit like her?" However, using Alice as a model has the potential to backfire for three reasons:

1. These comparisons do not really help children understand what Alice is doing that the teacher wants others to emulate. The teacher might like that Alice is sitting on the line on the carpet, but another child might notice instead that Alice is doing something with her hands and decide to emulate that.

2. Alice may feel embarrassed by the spotlight. Some people are not comfortable being singled out and having their behavior highlighted as an example for all. If Alice is uncomfortable with the attention, she may begin to misbehave so that she no longer finds herself in that embarrassing situation. Alice might also begin to measure her worth based solely on her compliance. She may feel an unhealthy pressure to always be "good" and worry that others may not value or like her if she does not meet behavioral expectations.

3. Other children may grow to resent Alice and the fact that the teacher holds her up as an example. Especially in classrooms of older children, others may begin to pick on Alice because of her favored position with the teacher.

Also, when teachers use phrases such as, "I like the way Alice is sitting" in this way, they are really using a form of coercion and provocation. Instead of encouraging cooperation, statements like this can cause classrooms to become places of competition as children strive to become the object of the teacher's attention. They don't copy the behavior because of social understanding or intrinsic motivation, but because they crave the attention of a caring adult. When children are not receiving that attention for following social rules, they will often look for other ways, some negative, to gain the attention they long for.

As with the other techniques in this section, comparisons may produce short-term compliance, but they do not set children up for long-term success in understanding how to be a member of a classroom community.

Rewards

Often, a child's day in the classroom ends with a sticker or special treat if he had a "good" day. Teachers and parents try to prompt desired behavior with the promise of rewards. Author and educator Alfie Kohn, in his book *Punished by Rewards*, makes the case that children are harmed as much by rewards as they are by punishments. Both are ways to control and manipulate children and are often distributed without the child being able to connect the result with what he did to deserve it. If a child cannot connect his behavior with the reward, the reward is ineffective as a teaching tool.

What does a *good day* mean? Is there a balance sheet? A child may think, "Mostly, I was good, but I did get frustrated and hit the child who was trying to eat off my plate. Is that a good day?" Or, at the opposite end of the scale, she may think, "I did not cooperate during circle time and I threw a fit when it was time to come back inside. I was noisy during nap and cranky afterward because I did not sleep. But, when I saw the stickers come out, I ran and gave the teacher a hug and showed him how I could sit like a good girl. Is that a good day?" Rewards come from a place of power, and the person with the stickers has the power to decide, without explanation or teaching of alternatives, what constitutes a "good day." Those who receive a sticker can wear it like a badge of honor, and those who don't are left simmering in the injustice of the situation.

Rewards are often used to encourage children to behave in a certain way. "Sit at circle time or you will not get a sticker today" may work temporarily. But at some point, especially if the promise of a sticker is used throughout the day, a child is going to decide that the required task is not worth the promised reward. Typically, if a circle time is engaging and fun, a child won't need the assurance of a sticker to stick around to see what happens.

In the long term, rewards can actually backfire. Children can become dependent on a reward. They may even come to expect a reward for behaviors they previously engaged in without affirmation or reward—behaviors they were already intrinsically motivated to do. If everyone gets a sticker for taking a nap, for example, children who naturally would have been compelled to sleep because they are tired may resist that urge until they know the reward is forthcoming. In this case, the reward serves to lessen motivation in the long run. As Kohn states, "I want [a student] to share her pleasure with me, not look to me for a verdict. I want her to exclaim, 'I did it!' instead of asking me uncertainly, 'Was that good?'"[16]

Empty Threats

"If you guys don't stop messing around, I am canceling the Halloween party next week." "I will take all the toys out and you will have nothing left to play with if you don't clean up this room right now."

From a place of deep frustration, words like these have emerged from many a teacher's lips. (I myself am guilty as charged.) Unfortunately, these types of threats do very little to change children's behaviors or to teach them necessary social skills.

Most of the time, children recognize when a teacher has no intention of following through on the promised action. They know that she will not empty the room of materials, and they know that teachers live for party days as much as, if not more than, children do.

If these empty threats have an impact, it is on the children who are *not* challenging social norms. Children who consistently follow the rules may feel unfairly targeted, as they fear they will pay the price for misdeeds they did not commit.

As with many of the other strategies discussed here, this response to challenging behavior may inspire a momentary reprieve, but it does not provide children with any information about the behaviors the teacher wants to see instead.

Sending Children to the Office or Home

In many cases, children exhibit challenging behaviors in response to the social stresses and demands of the early childhood classroom. It is the reality of today's world that a lot of children spend much of their time enclosed in four walls, separated from their primary caregivers. For many, the stress of being in this environment, surrounded by so many other children and having to follow an externally dictated routine, becomes too much and they lose control.

In these cases, removing a child from the situation by sending him to the director's office or calling family members to take him home can provide a temporary respite from the situation. And, much of the time, the child may stop the behavior when he is removed from the classroom. However, this response does little to teach the social skills the child needs to succeed in the classroom, and it may ultimately backfire in the long run.

Sometimes, hanging out with the director is fun. A child gets lots of attention that does not have to be shared with anyone. And, for many children, the idea of being sent home to be with the adults they love most in the world is the ultimate prize. If children learn that by misbehaving they can obtain their goals, they may resort to these behaviors more and more often. Instead of helping a child succeed in the classroom, this response can lead to more challenging behaviors.

Sometimes a child may need to be removed from the classroom for the safety of others or for the mental health of the teacher. While removal may be necessary during these times, it is important that it be used as sparingly as possible and with the understanding that it's not effective in teaching a child the skills she needs to be successful in the early learning environment.

THE BENEFITS OF BREAKS

In some cases, a child's behavior is communicating that the classroom situation is too much for him. It can help to provide this child with breaks throughout the day before he loses control, not in response to challenging behavior. For example, if a child usually loses control at cleanup time, a member of management or another teacher can remove the child from the classroom before cleanup time and return with him as it is ending, showing him how to help so he can be successful.

If teachers are in tune with children, they may notice when children start to get overwhelmed. At these times, teachers can use a code word to alert another staff member to come for the child or to help with the classroom so the teacher can take the child for a quick walk around the center to help relieve some of the stress. Together, the adult and child can come up with a plan to help the child reintegrate into the classroom after the walk. In these instances, removing a child from the classroom is not a response to challenging behavior, but rather a proactive strategy to help the child be successful.

Calling Family Members

At all educational levels, communication between educators and family members is essential. This is especially true in the early childhood years. Open lines of communication benefit the classroom and the family, particularly the child. However, while open communication is a hallmark of the preschool classroom, calling families in response to challenging behaviors can be counterproductive.

When teachers call parents regarding behaviors a child displays in the classroom, they are essentially putting the child in a situation in which she can be punished twice for the same offense—once at school and once at home. This is especially unfair in response to the mistaken behaviors introduced on page 78. When a behavior is not ongoing or damaging to the child or others, a teacher can deal with it at school without involving families in further consequences.

Notifying family members (or threatening to) often compels family members to discipline children at home for challenging behaviors that occurred at school. While teachers and parents do this with the best of intentions, it often has little effect on children's behaviors. Young children have a limited ability to connect actions and consequences, especially when they are separated by long periods of time. And for a young child, even a couple of hours is a long time. If children are punished at home in the evening for something that happened during the school day, it is very unlikely to have an impact on their behavior. They are unable to understand a consequence administered so long after a behavior occurred. Nor will they moderate a behavior based on the threat of a consequence that will occur so far in the future, like when they get home that evening.

Home consequences also do not help children learn the social skills they need at school. At home, most children do not have to share materials, space, and attention with so many other children. Also, young children learn social skills in the moment, not through conversations before or after the incident. Unless the same social situations are occurring at home, it is very difficult for families to help children develop the skills they need in classroom situations.

Moreover, by calling family members in response to behaviors, teachers may end up losing some of the child's respect and trust. If a teacher consistently calls a child's parents to deal with his behaviors, the child may come to believe that the teacher lacks the knowledge or the skills to deal with these social indiscretions alone. Once firm in this belief, the child may come to reject the teacher's attempts at guidance.

While calling families will not impact a child's behavior in the classroom, it is important to partner with them when dealing with challenging behaviors, especially if the behavior is ongoing and occurs both at home and at school. Ongoing conversations that bring families and teachers together to discuss the challenges, seek solutions, and make sure everyone is on the same page are important. As opposed to simply informing a family of a child's behaviors, these conversations bring them in as equal partners in supporting the child's experience in the classroom. We will look more at collaborating with families to help a child be successful in the classroom in chapter 7.

Removing Objects

In the early childhood classroom, children commonly argue over a desired object. Sharing is hard, even for adults. And in the world of early education, children are put in a situation where nothing in a classroom belongs to them and they are required to share everything for forty to fifty hours a week. Often, the easiest response to this situation is to remove the disputed object with a concise, "I will put this away until you learn how to share." Of course, it is impossible to learn how to share if the object you need to share is no longer in the picture.

As with the other responses discussed here, this reaction may solve the problem for the time being, but it does nothing to teach children the skills they need to successfully share and cooperate in the classroom. Teachers can use these skirmishes to help children learn how to navigate conflicts—a skill that will serve them well beyond the classroom as they enter a world where compromise and sharing are daily requirements.

Removing Privileges

So often when children are exhibiting challenging behaviors, it is because they are, in fact, children. They have not yet developed the ability to control their impulses and natural energy in a classroom setting. At times, in response to challenging behaviors, teachers remove desired activities, such as being allowed to go outside with other children, getting a turn to take home the class teddy bear, or sharing something during show-and-tell. They feel that if children lose access to an activity they enjoy, they will behave in socially acceptable ways in their desire to win back the activity.

In reality, this is one of the most ineffective approaches to troubling behaviors. For instance, if the need to burn off energy is at the root of a behavior, denying a child access to activities that will burn off that energy is sure to backfire. Often children who are exhibiting challenging behaviors need even *more* opportunities to be active and run, jump, climb, and spin, not fewer. Instead of taking away access to large-muscle play from these children, teachers can reduce problem behaviors by increasing their access to these activities (see figure 1.4 on page 44).

Likewise, when we take away important experiences like bringing home the class teddy bear or being able to share at show-and-tell, we erode our relationship with the child, which can lead to more challenging behaviors. As discussed in chapter 3, building relationships with children and helping them feel like a valued part of the community is essential in creating a responsive and appropriate classroom.

Many of the responses to challenging behaviors just discussed have been used for ages in early childhood classrooms in all parts of the world. Many of them are used in frustration, and teachers are at a loss for how to support children who act out in the classroom. Although these responses may feel familiar or comfortable, they don't help children learn social skills. Next, we will look at responses that help children learn the social skills they need to effectively navigate the classroom environment.

Effective Ways to Respond to Challenging Behavior and Teach Social Skills

When a gardener is faced with a plant that does not blossom, he does not seek to punish the plant. Instead he looks for tools to guide the plant toward healthy growth. Likewise, when a child exhibits a challenging behavior that suggests she may lack some of the skills she needs to be in a classroom environment, the teacher focuses on responses that guide and teach the child. Let's look at some responses that are effective in helping children learn necessary social skills.

Redirection

At its base, *redirection* means to move children's attention and energy from an undesired behavior to one that is more acceptable. When a child is tearing books, for instance, she may be indicating a desire to rip paper. Tearing is not in itself a challenging behavior. In fact, when children tear, they are coordinating movements and strengthening the muscles they need to hold a pencil. Instead of stopping the behavior, a teacher can help redirect the child to a more appropriate expression of it. For example, fill a tub with papers donated by families. When a child tears a book, a poster, or some other inappropriate item, a teacher can nurture social skills by responding, "If you tear that book, we cannot enjoy the story anymore. Please put it down. I have a whole bunch of paper you can tear over here." (See figure 1.4 on page 44 for other ideas for how to redirect children's physical energy in acceptable ways.)

When teachers redirect children's natural urges into acceptable expressions of those urges, they are providing the social understandings children need to keep themselves and others safe. By redirecting children, teachers can help them differentiate between appropriate and inappropriate expressions of desired behaviors.

Clearly Define Desired Expectations

At times, children exhibit challenging behaviors simply because they do not understand the expectations for being part of a social group in an early childhood classroom. We can't hold children accountable for expectations they do not comprehend. To teach children social expectations, teachers must clearly state and define them in ways that children understand.

Following are strategies to accomplish this. One is proactive and the other is reactive, but both serve the same purpose: to help children learn social expectations. The first proactive strategy helps clarify acceptable behaviors for children. This is especially important at the start of a school year or when there is a large transition of children into a new classroom.

Share Stories

Some of the behaviors we expect from children are clear to adults, but children have not yet mastered them. Stories have great power in helping children learn these skills.

Many storybooks have been written about what children can expect in the classroom and how they are required to behave. Reading these books with children can help them learn through the experiences of the characters. As teachers read the story, they can facilitate discussions about what is happening in the book and help children connect it with what is expected of them in the classroom. Through conversations with children, teachers might also share their own stories of learning to navigate social expectations.

Teachers can also help children create stories based on children's own experiences in the classroom. Using pictures of children to make books about social expectations is a powerful teaching tool. Let's look at mealtimes and naptimes for examples of how this might play out in practice.

The ways children eat meals are as unique as the families into which they are born and may vary from day to day. Some children sit with their families and eat around a table. Some may eat on a couch while watching TV. Some eat in the backseat of a car as they travel from one activity to another. Some eat from an adult's plate as the child and adult sit together. Some eat at a kitchen island while the adults do chores or other work. And still others may eat while walking around the house. Yet when children come to school, teachers often expect that all children know how to sit in a chair surrounded by other kids, eat only from their plates, and stay seated until the meal is complete. Teachers can demonstrate and model meal expectations for children. They can also outline meal expectations through pictures and words in a class mealtime book. (See information about expectations books on pages 46–47.) By reading this story with children as they transition into the classroom, a teacher provides them with the knowledge they need to be successful in this social expectation.

This technique may also be helpful to set expectations for naptime. Again, children have many different sleeping arrangements at home. Some sleep in a dark room by themselves, some share a family bed, some fall asleep on a couch and are transferred to bed, and some may fall asleep while watching a favorite movie or TV show. I knew one father who had to walk up and down a hallway with his daughter in a back carrier to get her to sleep each night. Yet, when children come to school, they are expected to lie on a cot or mat in a well-lit room, usually with their shoes on and with lots of other children and activity surrounding them. To help them adjust, teachers can work with children to make a book titled *Naptime at School*. Each page can show a child modeling what it means to put the blanket on the cot, to lie still, to breath deeply, to think relaxing thoughts, and so on (see page 46). The book can provide clear guidance for what teachers mean when they instruct children to rest.

Reading and sharing stories (published or class-created) with children is a proactive strategy to teach social skills. It presents children with knowledge before they encounter new situations that may prove challenging for them. Teachers can share or create as many books as needed as new situations present themselves.

They can expand on the stories with puppets, discussions, or dramatic play situations that support children in processing and applying what they learn.

These stories can also be shared in response to problem behaviors. If a child is struggling in a social situation, the teacher can remind him of the characters in a story shared previously. Teachers can reread books with children in small groups or individually to help bolster the skills needed to manage new or stressful social expectations.

The world of stories is a powerful one for children. By sharing stories with children, we arm them with the knowledge they need to thrive in the social life of the classroom, and especially in situations that differ from their home lives.

Intentionally Teach Expectations

Teachers create lesson plans to ensure that they are teaching the many academic skills children need to be successful students. They can use this same intentionality to help children gain the skills they need to navigate the social expectations of the early childhood classroom. What does it mean, for example, to "clean up" the block center? How do I "clear my plate" and "get ready for nap"? Unless teachers take the same deliberate approach to answering these questions as they do to planning lessons, some children may struggle to learn these skills through trial and error, or may not even attempt to learn them. In either case, the teacher will often perceive a challenging behavior when it is really a lack of understanding.

Along with sharing stories, teachers can cultivate social skills in children by planning activities around these skills. When teachers host small groups in the different areas of the classroom, they can play alongside children to model expected forms of play in that area. Teachers can also make a small-group game of cleaning up the area so children know how to meet this expectation.

To help children understand how to clear a plate, teachers can teach a song and sing along with children as they practice carrying dirty plates to a bucket. They can also make up songs to help children remember the steps in getting ready for nap. Music is a great way for children to remember steps in a process.

When teachers directly state and teach their expectations for classroom behaviors, children feel more confident in being able to meet those expectations. And children who feel confident are more likely to be successful and less likely to need to communicate through challenging behaviors.

Natural and Connected Consequences

The word *consequences* can evoke strong reactions in some people. The idea of consequences is often conflated with the idea of punishment since both are commonly delivered by someone in power to another person in reaction to an undesired behavior. In this context, the *natural* consequences are the events that happen naturally as a result of a behavior. For example, if a child puts a large block on top of a narrow tower, the block will probably fall. *Connected* consequences are those that help children connect their actions with a result so they can learn. For example, if a child spills sand from the sand table, she can help clean it up as a connected consequence and also as a way to fix the problem.

Neither natural nor connected consequences are designed to be punitive (in fact, a natural consequence is not even designed, it is simply the result of an action). They instead help children learn as they connect their behaviors with the outcomes of those behaviors.

Many adults can foresee the consequences of a behavior. It's often an adult's instinct to want to protect children from these consequences by stopping them from engaging in the behavior or by negating the consequences following it. In some cases, this is wise—especially if the consequence is harmful to the child or others, expensive, or too far in the future to really have an impact on the present. For example, the natural consequence of a child throwing a ball at a window could be that the window breaks. However, it is better to stop the behavior to avoid this expensive and dangerous consequence rather than use it as a teaching tool. Likewise, the natural consequence of not washing his hands might be that a child gets sick or spreads an illness. This consequence is often too difficult for children to connect to their actions and may occur too far in the future for them to comprehend. Yet preventing illness is so important that it's better to simply require handwashing and help children understand and meet the expectation.

Still, in many cases, consequences can help children learn valuable social skills. For example, if a child says something that hurts another child's feelings, the second child may not want to play with her anymore. Sometimes teachers will step in and say something like, "Oh, she didn't mean it" or, "Say you're sorry, and we can all be friends again." With this response, it is harder for children to learn that being unkind can have unpleasant consequences. If, instead of protecting children from these consequences, teachers help them understand how their behaviors led to the situation, children are more likely to adopt socially acceptable behaviors. Teachers can facilitate this understanding with words like, "He doesn't want to play with you right now because you said something that made him sad. Let's find something else to do for a little while. We can come back later and talk about how you can help him feel better." After a little time has passed, the teacher can help the first child reenter the social situation.

If we want children to make good choices when they are older, they must be able to consider the consequences of those choices. Teachers can support children in developing this skill by helping them connect their actions with consequences when both the children *and* the possible consequences are smaller.

Repetition, Consistency, and Modeling

Children learn through repetition, by revisiting concepts in a variety of ways and in a variety of settings. Teachers would never expect a child to learn to count after one exposure to numbers. Nor can we expect them to learn that they need to sit while eating lunch, not to touch the hair of the child next to them, and other social expectations after just one admonishment. For children to learn appropriate classroom behaviors, teachers need to be consistent and repetitive when guiding them. Teachers also need to address the behaviors every time children exhibit them. It is very confusing for children when teachers tell them one day that they can't run in the classroom but the next day the running is ignored.

Children are also more likely to adopt desired social behaviors when teachers model their stated expectations. If teachers tell children they cannot climb on shelves, but teachers often sit or lean on shelves, there is a disconnect between the verbal and observed expectation. If teachers expect children to sit at a table while eating, but teachers eat while walking around, children are more likely to copy what they *see* rather than what they are told.

Choose Your Battles

Children have a lot to remember when it comes to the rules they must follow as part of a classroom community. Obviously, all children are not going to follow all the rules all the time. So teachers need to decide which rules are the most important for a child's well-being and focus on those, especially if the child is struggling with multiple challenging behaviors. "Choosing your battles" means that instead of trying to correct all behaviors at the same time, you look at challenging behaviors along a continuum. When a child is displaying many challenging behaviors, a teacher focuses on those that are detrimental to the physical safety of the child or others and ignores the ones that are not.

A child loses confidence and a positive sense of self if she is constantly hearing "no" and if most interactions with teachers are focused on how she is failing. Teachers can instead overlook those behaviors that are disturbing but not unsafe. Some examples of these behaviors might include not wanting to participate in group activities, showing mild disrespect, or not helping clean up. In the grand scheme of things, these behaviors, while frustrating, are less disruptive than others to the well-being of the classroom community. It is better to ignore these and focus on behaviors that are truly unsafe, such as running in the classroom, hurting others, or throwing toys. Once these more harmful behaviors are under control, teachers can direct their attention to the less disruptive ones.

When children are struggling in the classroom, they probably already feel like they are failing. They may be confronted by the failure every day in the disappointed faces of their teachers, the serious lectures from their parents, and the exclusion by their peers. The more they hear "no," the more frustrated they might feel for failing, and the more they might choose to act out that frustration. Hence, the cycle of failure becomes self-perpetuating. If a child internalizes the image of himself as a failure, that image becomes his reality. Once that self-image becomes his truth, he is less likely to be able to break out of the cycle. By focusing on only those behaviors that truly disrupt, while also regularly acknowledging desired behaviors, a teacher helps break the cycle of failure, thus giving the child a chance at success.

When three-year-old Jess came to Ms. Leesa's classroom, she had already been kicked out of three preschool programs. Her mother cried as she listed the behaviors that resulted in her daughter's most recent expulsion. She recounted the many times she was called to the center to pick up an out-of-control Jess. At the end of her visit with Ms. Leesa, Jess's mom resignedly told the teacher she expected that in four weeks her daughter would be expelled again and that she was just trying to piece together childcare until Jess started public school so she wouldn't lose her job.

In looking at the documentation from other centers, Ms. Leesa could see that Jess did struggle in social situations. When frustrated or angry, she often hit and kicked teachers and other children. But Ms. Leesa also noticed that most of Jess's tantrums grew out of relatively minor offenses—for example, not wanting to be at circle time, not helping clean up, and saying words like *stupid*. Ms. Leesa and her director came up with a strategy of only asking Jess to comply with rules that were truly important for her safety or the safety of the classroom.

Jess's first weeks in the classroom were challenging for her, Ms. Leesa, and her classmates. As Jess had come to see herself as a failure in a classroom setting, she challenged expectations at every turn. Ms. Leesa and her co-teachers picked their battles and only stepped in when the behaviors put Jess or others in danger. They ignored smaller misdeeds and took every opportunity to affirm Jess's positive behaviors. For example, Ms. Leesa noticed that Jess came into the classroom one morning and went to wash her hands without being reminded. While Jess was washing her hands, the teacher got down on her level and said, "Thanks for washing your hands, Jess. You know how to keep yourself healthy." Another time, the co-teacher noticed Jess jump up to get some paper towels when a classmate spilled milk at lunch. The co-teacher acknowledged the action, saying, "You were so quick to help, Jess. I bet Ava appreciated you helping her clean up."

Jess still had very little interest in circle time and was not much help during cleanup, but the violent tantrums became a thing of the past as teachers made it easier for Jess to be successful. Using this strategy, they also helped Jess reshape the image she had of herself as a failure. Her general frustration with early childhood classrooms lessened, and the teachers helped give her positive ways to express her anger, which reduced incidents of lashing out at others. As Jess became more adept at navigating the social life of the classroom, teachers slowly introduced more expectations. When hurting others was no longer an issue, they moved on to using more appropriate language in the classroom. By choosing their battles, the teachers avoided situations in which Jess was more likely to react with a tantrum and set her up for success.

At times, teachers may feel that by ignoring small actions, they are letting children get away with undesired behaviors. In these situations, it is not about a child winning and a teacher losing: It is about setting the child up for success. The gardener is not concerned that by giving a plant what it needs to bloom, she is somehow giving in to the plant. Instead, she knows that by giving it what it needs, the plant will be more likely to flourish and grow to its potential.

In some situations, a teacher may be concerned that by letting one child get away with not cleaning up, other children may begin to exhibit the same behavior. For most children, however, the simple desire to be part of the classroom community and meet an adult's expectations is enough to drive positive behaviors. Especially if the expectations are seen as a positive as opposed to a negative (for example, if circle time is interesting and engaging and cleanup time is fun instead of a chore).

If children do complain that it's unfair how another child is being allowed to do something they are not, a teacher can respond by saying something like, "Fair doesn't mean that everyone gets the same thing. Fair means that everyone gets what they *need*. Right now, I am giving Kai what he needs. You don't need the same thing. Is there something you need?" Each child is an individual and has different needs. When a teacher shifts the focus from group management to individual guidance, children are more likely to respond positively to her interventions.

Acknowledge Effort

Part of helping children learn is encouraging, recognizing, and acknowledging their attempts to exhibit desired behaviors. Encouragement often includes empathizing with the difficulty some children may be encountering in a particular situation. When children are waiting in a hallway as they take turns using the bathroom before they go outside, a teacher might encourage them by saying, "You guys are becoming experts at waiting. I know waiting is hard. Who here thinks waiting is boring? Let's all growl to show how we feel about waiting. That felt good! Now, what song should we sing while we are hanging out here?" In this situation, the teacher is teaching the group about waiting by naming what they are doing, noticing that they are being successful, empathizing with their plight, providing them with an outlet for their frustration, and suggesting an activity to help make the waiting easier.

It is also important to notice and acknowledge when individual children are making strides in meeting social expectations. When acknowledging children's efforts, describe what you see them doing in detail. Teachers sometimes use phrases like "good job" and "that's nice" without much consideration. This type of casual praise is a common form of reward in many early childhood classrooms. Children can become dependent on these phrases, clamoring for a teacher's attention until the needed affirmation is issued. When a teacher offers a casual "good job" to a child, the phrase does nothing to indicate what he is doing that has drawn the teacher's approval. Instead, a phrase such as, "You are working so hard to eat the food just from your plate. Thank you," helps children understand how they are meeting the social expectations of the classroom.

As in all other areas of curriculum, teaching is more effective when teachers are clear and direct as they introduce expectations for children and as they acknowledge children's efforts in meeting those expectations.

Interrupt Behaviors

Sometimes children give physical or other indicators that challenging behaviors are about to happen. A child may tense her shoulders before throwing inappropriate objects or may utter a particular phrase before dissolving into a violent tantrum. These indicators give teachers a chance to interrupt the behavior and distract the child. For example, a teacher may notice a girl tensing her shoulders just before she is about to throw a chair. The teacher can step in and stop the behavior by saying, "It looks like you are getting angry. Put the chair down.

That is not safe. I bet we can find something positive to do with that anger. Would you like to throw socks or run in place with me?" Without directly addressing the potential chair throwing, the teacher is providing an acceptable behavior to replace the unsafe one. The teacher is also sending the message that being angry is okay, as long as it is expressed in ways that do not injure oneself or others or damage materials.

For some behaviors that are very frequent, teachers may need to temporarily shadow children. Shadowing increases the chance that a teacher will be close by to stop the behavior as it is about to happen. This is a particularly good strategy for toddlers who are biting. When a teacher is close, she can simply redirect a child when he attempts to bite without even addressing the behavior. Children bite for a variety of reasons. When biting is chronic, it may be a habit—a way a toddler enters into play, tries to get a toy, expresses frustration, explores the world, or says, "I'm tired." By interrupting biting attempts, the teacher is breaking the habit in a gentle and supportive way. If the teacher recognizes a possible motivation for the bite, she can address it while redirecting the behavior. For example, "You want the ball? Let's find you another one."

With toddlers, it is not helpful to name the behavior as you interrupt it or to warn the child against the behavior if it does not occur. For example, with a child who bites, it is not necessary to name the biting behavior each time the shadowing teacher interrupts it. Instead, she can proactively provide the child with an alternate behavior before the biting occurs. With children over the age of three, a quick reminder that the behavior is inappropriate, such as, "Hands down. We don't hit people," serves to indicate what action you are stopping and why. Since the behavior did not happen, however, it does not serve to draw a child's full attention to it. Instead, the objective is for the child to understand the purpose behind the potential behavior. By focusing on the motivations behind behaviors instead of on the behaviors themselves, early care professionals are giving children the tools they need to navigate the social world of the classroom.

Teaching Steps in Conflict Resolution

As children spend eight to ten hours a day in the classroom, sharing space and materials with many other children, conflicts are inevitable. Along with helping children learn social skills and how to meet classroom expectations, teachers can create more peaceful classrooms by teaching healthy ways to address and navigate these conflicts.

Imagine a world in which all people had the ability to calmly and rationally negotiate their way through conflicts. How many shootings and other harmful situations would be avoided if all humans had this skill? Early childhood professionals are in a unique position to impact the future of our world as we help children traverse the numerous conflicts that arise each day. Teachers can help children learn the skills they need to be part of a classroom community, and the larger world community, by defining and guiding children through a consistent conflict resolution process.

At first, this process might seem cumbersome, since teachers must guide children deliberately through each step. After time and practice, however, teachers will find that children can navigate the process themselves, supporting each other through the steps as they move toward a resolution they can all support. Even two-year-olds can start to engage in a teacher-guided form of this process, with the teacher talking through each step and providing suggestions. And by the age of three or four, children can take a more active role in the process and learn the skills to resolve conflicts independently, or at least with less teacher guidance.

Step 1: Stop the conflict. When a conflict arises, move toward it, get down on the children's level, and neutralize the situation. This may mean calming down a child who is upset, separating children who are fighting, or holding onto a toy that is at the center of the conflict. Soothe children and say, "I am here to support you and I know we can work together to solve this."

Step 2: Understand the conflict. Assure children that they will all have the opportunity to state their sides of the story. Give each child time to recount what happened.

Step 3: Restate the conflict. Use as few words as possible to restate your understanding of what is at the core of the conflict. "So, what I hear is that you both need the yellow block. Is that correct?" If each child agrees, move on to the next step. If not, keep working the process until they all agree on the core of the conflict.

Step 4: Brainstorm and select a solution. Ask children for ideas about how they might resolve the conflict. This is a chance for them to verbally list any and all possible solutions, even if the solutions they suggest are unrealistic. In this step, the teacher's job is to listen and restate the ideas. Other children may also get involved with ideas at this step.

As children come up with solutions, check with the others to see if the solution is acceptable. For example, "Ahmad thinks that he should have the yellow block and you can use the blue one, Rachel. What do you think?" Rachel can say "no," at which point the teacher might say, "Rachel doesn't want the blue block. What other ideas might work?" And the process continues until children come up with a solution they all can accept.

If the process completely stalls, the teacher can step in to suggest ideas. For example, "What would you think about Rachel having the yellow block for five minutes? We can set a timer. Then, Ahmad, you would get it."

There also may be times when other children step in to help solve the conflict. For example, "Dwayne says that he can use the blue block and one of you can use the yellow block he has. Would that work?"

At times, one child may want to give up on the process. This is a legitimate choice as long as the child truly is content with walking away. For example, "Ahmad, are you sure you are okay with Rachel having the block and you going to another area? If not, I know we can find a solution together."

Step 5: Restate the solution. "So, Dwayne is going to use the blue block in his building and give his yellow block to Ahmad. Then both Rachel and Ahmad will have a yellow block. Is everyone good with that?" If all children are on board, the main part of the process comes to an end.

Step 6: Affirm the process. Once children have reached a solution, congratulate them on their work. Thank each child for working to find a solution. Some teachers encourage children to shake hands or thank each other for being part of the process.

Step 7: Follow-up. Once peace is restored, it is tempting to forget the situation so as not to remind children that there was a conflict. However, follow-up is an important step. It makes sure that everyone feels like they were heard and that the agreed-upon solution is still in place. After a few minutes, check in with each child with a comment like, "You did a great job working through that conflict. Thank you. Is everything still going okay?"

Let's look at this conflict resolution process in action.

A typical Tuesday morning in Ms. Shirley's classroom is shattered by loud voices erupting from the art center. Norah and Israel are pulling back and forth on a paintbrush as they struggle for a position in front of an easel. Ms. Shirley leaves the bingo game she is leading and heads quickly in that direction.

Ms. Shirley crouches down next to the children and puts her hand gently on the paintbrush. "It looks like we have a problem here," she says calmly. "I'm going to hold on to this while we work this out. I know we can figure out a solution together." Both children start talking at once. Ms. Shirley puts her arms around the children to calm them and says, "I get that you are both upset. Don't worry. I will make sure you each get a chance to talk. Norah, let's let Israel go first to tell me what is happening, then you will go. Israel, what happened?"

Israel responds that Malik, he, and Norah were in the art center when Malik said that he was going to paint at the easel. Israel said that he wanted to paint, too, but Norah jumped up and grabbed the paintbrush from the easel before he could get there. When Israel is finished, Ms. Shirley thanks him for telling his story, turns to Norah, and says, "Now, Norah, you tell us what happened." Norah tells a similar account, but says that she was already going to paint and that she got to the easel first. Ms. Shirley thanks Norah and says, "It sounds to me like you both want to paint at the easel. Is that correct?" Both children nod.

"Okay," continues Ms. Shirley, "we can figure this out. What ideas do you have for how we can solve this problem?" Norah speaks up and says, "I could go first, and Israel can wait until I am done." Israel shakes his head before she can even finish her sentence. Ms. Shirley says, "It looks like Israel doesn't like that idea. So let's keep going." Mai, who has stopped near the easel to watch the process, pipes in, "They could both paint together at the same time." Ms. Shirley smiles at Mai and says, "Thanks for trying to help, Mai." She looks at both children, "What do you guys think?" Norah says firmly, "I don't want to paint together. I want to paint by myself." Norah tries another solution, "Israel can paint a picture at the table. I will give him the red, green, and white paint." Ms. Shirley looks at Israel while he considers this. "What will I paint with?" he asks. Norah runs to the shelf, grabs another brush, and exclaims, "There is a brush right here." Israel again pauses. "I want the blue paint. You can keep the green," he says to Norah. Norah smiles and nods her head. "We can trade if we finish," she adds.

Ms. Shirley looks at both children. "Looks like we have a solution," she says, "I knew you could do it. Israel is going to paint at the table with the blue, red, and white paint. Norah will use the other colors at the easel. Are you both happy with that solution?" When both children nod, she continues, "Thanks for working this out. You came up with a creative solution. I'll check in with you in a couple of minutes to see how it is going." Norah runs to get a piece of paper for Israel while he puts on a smock. Ms. Shirley returns to her bingo game and then comes back in a few minutes to check in with the painters.

When conflicts arise, it may feel easier for teachers to just put the yellow block away or send both children away from the easel. However, neither of these responses teach children the skills they need to be successful in social situations. Conflict resolution takes time, practice, and patience. Teaching children a step-by-step process for addressing and resolving conflicts may not be the easiest response in the moment, but it will pay off mightily in the long run as children help each other solve problems peacefully and respectfully. Learning to resolve conflicts may be the one skill that best serves children as they make their ways as adults in the global community.

Chapter Summary

In the first few years of life, children are called upon to master a plethora of skills. They learn to move from place to place by walking upright, they learn to communicate in a way that others can understand, and they learn colors, shapes, numbers, letters, and all sorts of other things society deems important. In addition, children must also learn the skills they need to play and learn alongside others. When teachers look at challenging behaviors as a lack of social aptitude in many cases as opposed to willful misconduct, they can view these behaviors through a more forgiving lens. Learning to be part of a community is hard work. Early childhood classrooms can be compassionate laboratories in which children can learn these skills.

Like a gardener who provides a plant with extra fertilizer and supports while it grows, a teacher can see a child's lack of social understanding as an opportunity to teach and guide as opposed to a behavior to punish. When teachers move away from responses that do not effectively teach social skills and focus on those that do, they are more likely to give children the skills they need to succeed in the present classroom community and the future global community.

Chapter 5

The MoNSTeR Response:
Manage Unforeseen Events

Even the most proactive gardener must be diligent in observing how each plant in her care reacts to its circumstances. When a plant suddenly droops to the ground following a storm, for example, or loses leaves in reaction to a pest infestation, the gardener must move quickly and methodically to save it. Her immediate goal is to stabilize the plant so she can gather information that will inform her future interventions.

In a similar way, an early childhood teacher needs to be ever ready to respond to challenging behaviors that will inevitably occur in her classroom. The primary goal of a response should be to stop the behavior as quickly and calmly as possible, to protect all children involved, and to avoid the destruction of materials. An effective response also serves to reassure the child exhibiting the behavior, as well as the other children, and allows the teacher to gather information about what might be contributing to the situation. The MoNSTeR response to challenging behavior detailed in **figure 5.1** (see page 104) and the rest of this chapter allows teachers to meet all of these goals.

Some teachers may feel that this response lacks consequences for behaviors. It's true that the response itself has very little power in reducing a challenging behavior. A child will continue to communicate through that behavior until the reason for it is understood and the root cause addressed. *The function of a teacher's response is to stop the behavior, keep everyone safe, restore calm, and gather information about what might be causing the child to act in this way.*

Figure 5.1 The MoNSTeR Response to Challenging Behavior

Mo	N	S	Te	R
Move	**N**otice	**S**top	**Te**ach	**R**edirect
When a teacher sees a challenging behavior, the first step is to move calmly and quickly toward the situation. It can be helpful to issue a quick, reassuring self-affirmation, such as, "I can handle this," while in transit.	While responding to the behavior, the teacher notices whatever she can about the situation. What led up to the behavior? What might have caused it? What emotions does the child appear to be feeling? The answers will help the teacher understand the behavior so she can determine a plan to address it.	Once the teacher reaches the situation, the first step is to stop whatever is happening. This may entail gently stopping a child's arm from hitting, holding an object that is the cause of an argument, or removing a toy that is about to be thrown by a child.	As the teacher stops the behavior, she can take the opportunity to teach the child why the behavior is not acceptable in the classroom. The teacher should use as few words as possible to explain why she is intervening in the situation.	The final step is to redirect the child into a more appropriate behavior while delivering a short message on what is acceptable.

The MoNSTeR Response in Action

Let's examine a couple examples of what this response looks like in action.

Example 1: Jacob

Ms. Sherry notices that Jacob is getting frustrated in the dramatic play area. Suddenly, he yells and spins toward the pretend furniture, and she knows that sometimes Jacob pushes over items when he gets angry.

Mo = The teacher leaves the small math group she is leading and quickly **moves** toward the dramatic play area.

N = While hustling toward the situation, she takes **notice** of what might have caused Jacob's reaction. She notices that there is a pretend play jacket on the floor in front of him, with one sleeve turned inside out and a few of the small buttons still holding the front of the jacket closed. She also notices five or six children crowded into the dramatic play area, all dressed up in pretend play clothing and intently watching the situation unfold.

S = As Ms. Sherry arrives at the dramatic play area, she places herself between Jacob and the pretend refrigerator to **stop** him from pushing it over. She places her other hand gently on Jacob's shoulder to divert his attention from the situation to her.

Te = She crouches down so her face is even with Jacob's and **teaches** him firmly but with a concerned voice, "I can see you are angry, Jacob. Pushing furniture can tip it over and hurt someone, so I won't let you do that."

> **R =** Ms. Sherry continues and **redirects** him, "If you are angry, we can go throw socks at the wall. Or, I can help you solve the problem with this jacket. Which do you prefer?"
>
> Jacob chooses to throw balled-up socks at the wall until he is a little calmer. Once he is calm, Ms. Sherry talks with Jacob, starting the conversation with what she observed. "Throwing socks is a great way to get that frustration out. Thanks for making that choice, Jacob. I noticed the jacket in front of you over there. Were you frustrated because you could not get it on?" Jacob nods. Ms. Sherry puts her arm around him and asks, "Would you like me to help you, or would you like to go play somewhere else?" Jacob looks around the room and sees his friend Amy playing at the sensory table. He says that he would like to go play with her. Ms. Sherry accompanies him to the sensory table and helps him reenter play.

This response serves the classroom for many reasons:

1. It returns calm to the classroom, helping children know that the teacher is aware of what is happening and will work to keep everyone safe.

2. The teacher stops the child's behavior and teaches him a safe alternative.

3. The teacher can gather information about the situation and what may have caused the child's behavior.

    In this case, Ms. Sherry learns a couple of things about the classroom that she can adapt to help avoid a repeat of the situation in the future:

    • Ms. Sherry notes that many of the pretend play clothes may be difficult for children to take on and off. She makes sure to find some that do not have buttons or ties and may be easier for children to manipulate.

    • Ms. Sherry also realizes that the dramatic play area has been exceptionally popular lately and that perhaps some overcrowding may have contributed to the conflict. She plans to increase the size of the area so it can accommodate more children.

    • Finally, she decides to implement a classroom management system so children can self-regulate the number of people who can be in each center at a time. Throughout the classroom, she adds signs that name the learning centers and show with dots how many children can safely play in the center. She introduces the concept to the large group and helps children learn to regulate themselves as they come and go from centers. This can also alleviate some of the overcrowding in the dramatic play area.

4. The child learns that the behavior is not appropriate, but he is not embarrassed or made to feel bad for struggling in the situation. Ms. Sherry can also gather information about Jacob and how he might need special supports in developing the social skills necessary to be successful in the classroom. Here are a few actions she takes on behalf of Jacob:

    • She creates a social story about frustration. A social story is a brief story that describes a situation and presents guidance in how children might respond in that situation. In this case, she creates a story with pictures and words that explains what the term *frustration* means, what it can feel and look like (she enlists other children to give examples of what it feels like to be frustrated), and examples and pictures of children in situations that may cause frustration and how they can safely express it.

- She also plans a couple of small-group activities that support the development of Jacob's fine-motor skills. She hopes that as he becomes more adept at manipulating small objects, he will have fewer frustrating experiences.

- Finally, Ms. Sherry and her co-teacher determine that they will work as a team to help develop Jacob's burgeoning social skills. Based on Vygotsky's theory of the zone of proximal development (see page 27) along with their observations of Jacob's developmental level, they plan experiences that are within his capabilities when he has the support of an adult.[17] They notice quickly if he starts to get frustrated and coach and guide him through the feeling.

By using the MoNSTeR response in this situation, Ms. Sherry supports the overall well-being of the classroom while providing Jacob with the special supports he needs to be successful in the community.

A NOTE ABOUT CLASSROOM MANAGEMENT SYSTEMS

Classroom management systems have begun to fall out of favor in some circles. Critics suggest that teachers respond to children's interests by expanding or contracting learning centers based on popularity. They claim that external limits imposed by management systems get in the way of children learning negotiation and problem-solving skills. While these skills are critical for children's long-term success, many young children do not come into the classroom prepared to navigate the complex world that is free choice or center time. Hence, center management systems can be a helpful short-term structure to support children in learning negotiation skills and conflict resolution. As they become more adept at these abilities, the teacher can begin to scale back the use of an external management system.

Example 2: Hazel

Let's look at another example of the MoNSTeR response in practice.

Mr. Darius and Ms. Stacey are co-teachers in a room with sixteen toddlers. Recently, one of the children, twenty-two-month-old Hazel, has been exhibiting a lot of biting, up to four times a day. Because of the frequency of the behavior, the two teachers work with the director to plan a schedule for shadowing Hazel. Both teachers will have periods of time during which they stay very close to Hazel to interrupt any biting attempts. They will also take notice of the circumstances surrounding the attempts so they can determine a plan to address the behavior. During especially busy times of the day, for example, the transition from lunch to nap, a member of management or a floating staff member will step in to help in the classroom or to remove Hazel for a walk around the center whenever possible.

Mo = Because Mr. Darius and Ms. Stacey are always close to Hazel, they can physically **move** themselves between her and other children when she tries to bite.

N = Also, because the teachers are very focused on Hazel, they are hyperaware of the circumstances leading to each biting attempt. They **notice** how Hazel reacts to different situations and can begin to hypothesize what may be causing the biting behavior. This knowledge will allow them to make a plan to address the circumstances behind the behavior so Hazel no longer needs to bite to communicate her needs.

S = Being near Hazel allows Mr. Darius and Ms. Stacey to intervene and **stop** any biting attempts before they happen. In most cases, they are able to anticipate when she is going to bite and can position themselves so that she is unable to hurt other children. The teachers can gently stop the biting without making Hazel feel bad for her behavior.

Te and R = As they interrupt the biting attempts, Mr. Darius and Ms. Stacey can **teach** Hazel the appropriate behaviors she needs to successfully interact with other children. Then, they can **redirect** her into those behaviors. For example, if she leans in to bite because she wants a piece of playdough another child has, Mr. Darius can place his hand between Hazel and the other child while saying, "It looks like you want some playdough Hazel. Let's ask Mateo if you can have some." Or, "I have some more playdough right here that you can have, Hazel." Over time, Hazel learns skills she can use to be successful in the classroom community without being punished or separated from the group.

THE ROLE OF CONFLICT RESOLUTION IN THE MONSTER RESPONSE

Often, conflicts between children are at the heart of a child's outburst. She may feel frustrated, angry, or hurt during struggles over materials, attention, and shared space. Challenging behaviors are often the result of a child being overwhelmed by these feelings and not knowing how to manage them.

As discussed in chapter 4, a consistent process to teach conflict resolution can provide children with the tools to address and negotiate conflicts that arise in a classroom setting. However, when a young child is in the midst of a challenging behavior caused by strong emotion, she is often not ready to go through a conflict resolution process.

In the example about Jacob, if his frustration had been due to a conflict with another child over the jacket, once he was in that state, any attempt to help him immediately resolve the conflict would likely have been futile and only added to his frustration. Ms. Sherry would still need to stop Jacob from pushing over the pretend furniture and then provide him with an acceptable outlet (throwing socks at the wall) for his emotion. Once he is calm, she could say to him, "It looks like you were angry because Amy took the jacket you were going to wear. Shall we go back and figure out that situation with her, or would you like to do something else?" If he chooses to go back to the conflict, she could then try guiding him through the process of conflict resolution with Amy. In this way, Ms. Sherry first addresses and defuses the challenging behavior and then moves on to coach Jacob in resolving conflicts.

Chapter Summary

When teachers use the MoNSTeR response, they are strategically addressing challenging behaviors in a way that teaches as opposed to punishes and seeks to understand rather than ostracize. How teachers respond in this approach remains consistent for *all* behaviors—from swearing to biting to destroying materials. All of these behaviors are ways children communicate, and they will continue until the communication is understood and addressed.

Remember, the power to change behaviors generally does not come from how teachers respond to a behavior in the moment. Instead, it comes from understanding the motivations driving the behavior. Like the steadfast gardener's dedication to realizing each plant's potential, the MoNSTeR response allows teachers to gather necessary information and adapt the environment or enact strategies to teach social skills so each child can be successful in the classroom community.

Chapter 6

Unmet Social and Emotional Needs:
Pay Special Attention to Faltering Flowers

The committed gardener proactively prepares the earth so the sowed seeds have every opportunity to bloom. During the growth process, the gardener monitors the plants and provides any extra supports they need to flourish. Despite the gardener's valiant efforts, however, some plants still may need specific attention to reach their full potential. A plant that bends in response to fattening buds may need a trellis, or one that withers in the shadow of a larger bloom may need to be moved to a sunnier spot in the garden. Similarly, even if a dedicated teacher sets up classrooms responsive to children's developmental and learning needs, builds supportive relationships with children and families, and uses appropriate methods to teach needed social skills, some children may still struggle to be successful in the classroom setting. In these special cases, children are often reacting to a situation, in school or at home, in which their social and emotional needs are not being met. This situation may be temporary, such as when a child is staying with an aunt because Mom is in the hospital, or due to long-term circumstances, such as when a child has lost both parents in a car accident and is now being raised by a loving but distracted older sibling.

In this chapter, we will examine the social-emotional needs that all people have and how those needs can be at the root of children's challenging behaviors if they are not met. We will also look at what teachers can do to meet these needs in the experiences they plan, the spaces they design, and how they interact with children. As Frederick Douglass said, "It is easier to build strong children than to repair broken men." When the adults in a child's life consistently meet his social-emotional needs, they raise a strong, resilient child. It is much more effective to remedy unmet needs in a child's early years—and set him back on a path of healthy growth—than to wait until he is grown and more set in his ways.

Behaviors That Require an Intentional Response

Most of the time, as we've discussed in previous chapters, children's challenging behaviors communicate that there is a mismatch between their needs and classroom factors or that the child needs to learn certain social skills. However, at times challenging behaviors call for more intentional responses from a teacher. To determine if a behavior falls into this category, ask the following questions:

Does the behavior frequently put the safety of the child, other children, or staff at risk? Keeping all children physically and emotionally safe is job number one for the early childhood professional. If a child's behavior occurs often and that behavior puts someone's safety at risk, a teacher will need to come up with a plan to address the situation.

Is the child harmed emotionally by the behavior? Sometimes a behavior may not have much of an impact on other children, but it may lead to emotional harm for the child exhibiting it. It may lead to other children ostracizing the child or staff having a negative reaction to her. Frequent tantrums, difficulty sharing, or continual whining might fall into this category. Over time, the child exhibiting the behavior may come to see herself as "bad" and be hurt that other children or teachers react negatively to her.

Do other adults see the behavior as challenging? At times, certain behaviors may irk one teacher, but other adults may not be bothered by them. In those situations, the teacher and child may be involved in an ongoing power struggle or the behavior in question may be pushing a teacher's "hot button" (see sidebar on page 111). Or, if the behavior only occurs with the same adult, it is likely due to a factor related to that teacher—for example, the teacher has inappropriate expectations. For a behavior to require an intentional, individual response, it typically needs to be experienced and seen as challenging by more than one adult.

Does the behavior occur in various settings and at various times during the day? Along with being experienced by more than one adult, a behavior in this category occurs in a variety of situations. If the behavior consistently occurs at the same time of day, it is probably due to a classroom factor or a child needing some special supports to learn social skills. For example, if a child consistently throws a violent tantrum during circle time, the behavior is probably due to the expectations around that activity. By adjusting those expectations, the behavior will usually go away. Similarly, if a toddler only bites in the half hour before lunch, it could be that he is trying to communicate that he is hungry. Simply giving him a small snack midmorning may eliminate the biting behavior. However, if observation shows that the behavior occurs throughout the day in different settings, the child may need some more intentional supports.

Behaviors in this category are still being used by the child as a form of communication, but the teacher's responses to them should be more individualized and intentional. Since the behaviors are due to unmet social-emotional needs, the teacher will need to determine a plan to meet those needs so the behavior is no longer necessary.

TEACHERS HAVE HOT BUTTONS, TOO!

Teachers are human beings, and it is impossible to turn off personal preferences and pet peeves just because one is responsible for the care and education of a group of children. In the classroom, these pet peeves are often referred to as *hot buttons*. Children's behaviors that are viewed as particularly egregious by one teacher may not even register as a challenge to another.

For example, when I was a teacher I had a hard time with whining. It grated on my nerves and pushed every button I had. I could keep my calm when children threw furniture, swore, or had violent tantrums, but in the face of whining, I could feel my blood pressure rising and I just wanted to whine right back. In reality, whining is no better or worse than other challenging behaviors children exhibit. It was just more difficult for me as it pushed my hot button.

Feelings are neither right nor wrong. They are simply reactions to outside stimuli. Just like children, we cannot control our feelings, but we can control how we express our feelings and react to others' behavior. It is important that teachers recognize their hot buttons, so they can acknowledge how certain behaviors might compel strong reactions and can intentionally work to control these reactions.

For behaviors that push your hot buttons, a few strategies can be helpful:

- Be honest with yourself and others about your hot buttons.

- Recognize that a behavior that pushes your hot buttons is about you, *not* the child.

- Communicate with a co-teacher. Have a code word that lets her know you need support in addressing a behavior that feels especially challenging to you. She can also use the code word to let you know when you need to walk away from a situation.

All teachers have hot buttons. For one, it might be children misusing materials. For another, it could be children refusing to eat food put on their plates. In many cases, a hot button is related to something from the adult's childhood and upbringing. As teachers reflect on the topic of challenging behaviors, understanding and acknowledging their own hot buttons is an important part of the process.

Human Social and Emotional Needs

As humans, we all have certain social and emotional needs. The intensity of these needs may vary at different times of life and across personalities, but we all have them to varying levels. Children, of course, also have these needs. (A reproducible page detailing children's basic social-emotional needs is included in the appendix on page 169.) At times, their challenging behaviors communicate that these basic social and emotional needs are not being met by the circumstances of their lives. Let's look at these needs more closely.

The Eight Basic Social and Emotional Needs of Children[18]

1. **To be safe and secure.** Children need to feel that they are living and learning in a safe environment and that the adults in their lives are working to keep them from physical and emotional harm.

2. **To be loved and have a sense of self-worth.** As humans, we need to feel worthy of love. Every child deserves to feel like she is the center of someone's universe—that at least one adult absolutely adores her.

3. **To receive attention and be understood.** Often, we say of a child who is exhibiting challenging behaviors, "He just wants attention." In reality, attention is a need, not merely a want. Children need to feel that adults will pay attention to them and will work to understand their wants and needs.

4. **To have a sense of control and predictability.** Children need to feel like they have some control in their lives and that their days and nights will unfold with some predictability—for example, that the same people will be there to put them to bed, that the same smiling faces will greet them at school, and that Friday is family pizza day. Children feel more in control when they understand what is coming next and how the people around them will react to their behaviors. Routines, traditions, and rituals are important not only because they build cultural roots, but because they help create a sense of predictability and control.

5. **To recognize and be able to handle strong feelings.** Emotions are strange things. Even before we know what they are, they strongly impact our behaviors and the ways we interact with others. Children experience strong emotions in very physical ways—adrenaline might make them laugh or lash out, anger often causes their tummies to rumble, and sadness can make their chests ache and their eyes water. They experience these feelings, but may not yet be able to name them, let alone understand or manage them. Humans all have the need to be able to identify and control their feelings, as opposed to letting the feelings control them.

6. **To have a sense of power and feel independent and competent.** Children, like all people, need to feel that they have some power in their lives and that they can impact their present and future circumstances. This includes feeling like they are able to make decisions independently. Some people might refer to

this as a sense of self-efficacy—the belief that, when faced with a situation, a person will be able to handle it and work through it competently. Different from self-esteem—the belief that one is great just for being who she is—a healthy sense of self-efficacy helps children believe in their own competence and power in their lives.

7. **To be engaged in stimulating pursuits.** Our brains thrive on stimulation. Children need safe, engaging spaces to explore, interesting problems to solve, and fun "I wonder" questions to ponder.

8. **To enjoy relationships and have a sense of belonging.** Humans are social creatures. Studies show that people suffer when they are isolated and do better when they have at least one meaningful social relationship.[19] Children also need to feel like they belong and matter and that they are valued members of a community.

These eight needs are essential to a child's long-term well-being. When one or more of these needs are not being met, children will often communicate that lack through their challenging behaviors. As we've discussed, sometimes this lack might be temporary, such as when a family welcomes a new baby. A child's sense of control and predictability might be thrown for a loop as the family's life temporarily becomes very chaotic. In this case, a teacher may need to intentionally create an atmosphere that helps the child feel a sense of control and predictability while the situation at home stabilizes. Until the child feels this sense of control, the challenging behavior will likely continue.

At times, the behavior may communicate that a child's needs have not been met over a longer period. For example, a child who has been in and out of foster care may have a need to enjoy relationships and have a sense of belonging that is not being met. She may communicate her feelings of isolation and abandonment through challenging behaviors. Teachers will need to work especially hard to help her feel like she is an appreciated member of the classroom community. As her sense of belonging may have decreased over time, it will take time and intensive effort to rebuild it. But, until the child feels this sense of belonging, her challenging behaviors may continue to communicate her internal pain.

Determining Potential Causes for Unmet Needs

Now, let's look at some additional possible causes that result in each of these social-emotional needs being unmet, either temporarily or long-term. Note that all children are unique and differ greatly in how they respond to their circumstances. The chart in **figure 6.1** on page 114 lists triggers that might possibly result in unmet social and emotional needs. However, a trigger resulting in an unmet need is by no means a forgone conclusion. Some children face unbelievable trauma and come through relatively unscathed. Others react more strongly to temporary or long-term hardships. The chart is not meant to be diagnostic, but rather is meant to help teachers understand what may be at the root of a child's challenging behaviors in the classroom.

Figure 6.1 Possible Triggers for Unmet Social and Emotional Needs

UNMET SOCIAL-EMOTIONAL NEED	TEMPORARY TRIGGERS	LONG-TERM TRIGGERS
To be safe and secure	Accident Natural disaster Victim of a crime Sick parent Homelessness	Unsafe living conditions Abuse High-risk neighborhood Chronic illness Long-term homelessness
To be loved and have a sense of self-worth	Divorce New baby Failure to meet expectations (not being successful at toilet learning) Parent in a new relationship	Foster care Emotional abuse Demanding parent Conditional love
To receive attention and be understood	New baby Distracted family members (multiple jobs, in school) Speech delay Inability to communicate English language learner	Mentally ill caregiver Neglect Chaotic living situation
To have a sense of control and predictability	Deployed parent A move or a new living situation New baby Divorce or newly blended family Family member death	Chaotic living situation Mentally ill caregiver Abuse
To recognize and be able to handle strong feelings	Life changes that bring on strong emotions Sensory disorders	Emotionally volatile caregivers
To have a sense of power and feel independent and competent	Life change that makes the child feel powerless Not allowed to use new skills Transition to a new classroom Undiagnosed developmental delay	Child has no power Home has overly strict rules and consequences Always told "no" and criticized Treated like a baby
To be engaged in stimulating pursuits	Unengaging learning spaces Attention disorders	Strict household with no freedom Always told "no" Dangerous living situation
To enjoy relationships and have a sense of belonging	Family changes Transition to a new classroom	Foster care Chaotic family life Isolation from family members and friends

When young children do not have their social-emotional needs met, they will frequently externalize their internal pain through challenging behaviors. These behaviors indicate that something is broken in the child's world, and teachers need to be extra diligent in searching out ways to repair the hurt so the child no longer needs to act out to communicate his loss.

As you can see, many external factors can impact a child's social-emotional well-being. Many of the potential causes for these unmet needs overlap, so it is up to the teacher to figure out which need is most pressing for the child in that moment. Just as the gardener must look for clues as to why a plant is not thriving, the teacher must dig deep to figure out what need or needs are not being met. You can examine many factors to do this:

The child's emotions. While children are displaying challenging behaviors, it is important to note the feelings they seem to be expressing. While hitting another child, does the child look angry? Or does she express something that suggests the behavior is rooted in frustration or sadness? The emotions children convey can be an important clue about what is driving their behaviors.

When children are older, teachers can have conversations with them about what they are feeling. But even if they can talk about it, most children will still not be able to connect their feelings with their behaviors. After kicking three children, for example, Cody cannot say, "I am sad because my mom is working two jobs and I don't get enough of her attention, so I'm being mean to other children so my mom has to leave work to pick me up. Then I will have her attention." While he cannot express his motivations with such clarity, if a teacher asks, "You seemed really upset. Can you tell me about what you were feeling?" the child may be able to offer up some clues about how his emotions relate to the behavior. The teacher can add this information to other clues to determine how best to support the child. So, while Cody can't necessarily connect his behavior with feeling a lack of attention from his mom, he might look the teacher's way after kicking another child and say, "Are you going to call my mommy?" Or he might say, "I wish mommy would do this," as you rub his back at naptime. He might also play "mommy" in the pretend play center, line up the babies in front of the TV, and say, "You all be good for Auntie. I'm going to work. See you tomorrow." These behaviors and statements can be clues about the feelings that might be driving Cody's challenging behaviors.

Keep in mind that a young child's behaviors reflect his emotional reality. As adults, we have the ability to look at Cody's situation and provide perspective and context. *His mom is doing the best she can. At least Cody has a loving aunt who cares for him. When Mom does have a day off, she often volunteers in Cody's classroom.* This might lead a teacher, with the very best of intentions, to dismiss Cody's feelings with a quick hug and a comment such as, "You know your mom loves you." However, while all this may be true in context, Cody's reality is that he is not getting the attention he needs. As children get older, they gain the ability to take a different perspective and consider the context of a given situation. At that point, it can be appropriate to help a child see her reality in a different light. But as early childhood teachers, it is our job to understand a young child's reality and work to provide her with what she needs, as opposed to trying to convince her that what she feels is not legitimate.

Knowledge about the child. When teachers build strong relationships with children and families, they are more likely to understand what is happening in children's daily lives. Teachers can use this information to ascertain what may be driving a child's behavior. It is important to build these relationships over time, not only when children are struggling with challenging behaviors. If teachers wait until the challenging behaviors are already a problem, families may feel like they are being attacked or blamed for a child's behavior. At all times, the approach should be, "We all care deeply about this child and want the best for him. Let's work together to figure out how we can help." These conversations are not about assigning blame or judgment; they are about gaining information and determining how best to support a child and meet his unmet social and emotional needs. If a teacher knows what is happening in a child's life, she can use that knowledge to determine possible reasons for the child's behavior.

Contextual clues. As a teacher responds to challenging behaviors, it is important to observe what leads up to a behavior and what happens immediately after it. These clues can help a teacher decide what may be driving a child's behavior. Understanding the situations that trigger certain behaviors can provide important information about the child's motivations.

Experience and prior knowledge. While each child and situation is unique, teachers can draw on their knowledge of child development and similar past situations to try to understand what may be driving a child's current behavior. A teacher might have seen a similar situation in the past that helped him discover that when a child's parent gets remarried, the child may sometimes worry that there is no place for her in the new family. This need to have a sense of belonging might lead to challenging behaviors if it is not being met. So when Grace suddenly starts having outbursts in the classroom, based on the teacher's previous experience and knowledge, he might suspect that this new behavior is connected to the fact that Grace's dad just left on a honeymoon with his new spouse. The teacher can add this information to the other clues he has gathered as he seeks to interpret Grace's behavior.

As teachers observe, have conversations, and collect information, they can hypothesize as to what may be driving a child's challenging behaviors. Once a teacher has an idea about what the child may need, he can develop a plan to meet that need so the behavior is no longer necessary. A blank reproducible form that you can use to detail this plan is included in the appendix on page 174.

Planning to Meet a Child's Unmet Needs

The only way to address a behavior triggered by a child's unmet social-emotional need is to proactively meet that need so the behavior is no longer necessary. Teachers can do this through the experiences they plan, the environments they create, and the relationships they build with children. Over time, with intentional, individual intervention, a child's needs can be met in the classroom so that he can experience success.

Let's look at some ways that teachers can plan to meet children's unmet needs to alleviate challenging behaviors (see **figure 6.2**). Many of these interventions, while planned to help meet the social-emotional needs of an individual child, will benefit the whole class.

Figure 6.2 Strategies to Meet Children's Unmet Social and Emotional Needs

NEED	WAYS TO PROACTIVELY MEET THE NEED THROUGH . . .		
	Experiences	*Environments*	*Relationships*
To be safe and secure	Read stories about adults caring for children and what to expect in different situations (going to the doctor, having one's teeth cleaned). Provide opportunities for the child to journal so she can vocalize her fears and insecurities. Instead of discounting a child's feelings, teachers can affirm them and provide a listening ear.	Create calm "get away" areas that children can escape to as needed. Post pictures of children and their families. Provide a consistent routine and staffing so the child knows what to expect.	Let children have special security items (blankets, a shirt that smells like Mom, a teddy bear) in the classroom as needed. Model calmness and gentleness as much as possible. Provide physical touch and comfort if the child seems to need it (physical proximity during circle time, rubbing her back during naps, hugs throughout the day).
To be loved and have a sense of self-worth	Build "All About Me" boxes and books with children. Have family members write and leave notes for children to be read during the day. Help children write letters to their loved ones. Invite children's input and participation in planning experiences.	Incorporate materials in the classroom that reflect individual children's interests. Create separate spaces in the room where each child can display his work (instead of hanging all similar-looking art in one place).	Have caregivers leave personal materials (shirts or scarves that smell like them, extra keys) with children to reassure them that the adult will come back. Call children by their names and point out positive attributes of individual children. Encourage families to create hello and good-bye rituals at the start and end of each day.
To receive attention and be understood	Give children chances to take the lead in some experiences (choose how to move, pick which song to sing or story to read). Plan activities that invite children's participation (voting, child dictation, child input). During small-group activities, notice how children are using materials and reference this in conversations with individual children. For example, "That is cool how you are rolling the playdough into a long string, Erica. You have been working on that for a long time. Can you show me how to do that?"	Incorporate materials in the classroom that show you understand the child—items that reflect her interests. If the child is learning English, provide some books and pretend play materials from her native culture. If possible, a caregiver can record a story or song in the child's first language to be played at school.	Plan special times one-on-one with children. Be sure to spend one-on-one times with the child to give special attention when she's not exhibiting challenging behaviors. Shower attention on the child for positive behaviors. Provide two or three positive notes at the end of the day that families can celebrate with the child. If the child is an English language learner, learn and incorporate some words in her native language to help her feel comfortable. Get down on the child's level and practice active listening when she is speaking. Lean in, indicate with your body language that you are listening, and repeat what you hear her say.

Figure 6.2 Strategies to Meet Children's Unmet Social and Emotional Needs (continued)

NEED	WAYS TO PROACTIVELY MEET THE NEED THROUGH . . .		
	Experiences	*Environments*	*Relationships*
To have a sense of control and predictability	Create and post a pictorial schedule so children know what to expect. Be intentional about explaining expectations. Create social stories about school so children know what to expect. Plan open-ended experiences so children can make choices about how to use materials.	Have a predictable routine, give children notice if something is going to change. Refer children to a posted pictorial schedule. Provide pictorial schedules that children can carry so they know what to expect throughout the day. As they navigate the day, they can manipulate the schedule, maybe by removing pictures or moving a sticker to understand what has passed and what is coming next.	Have the same staff with children as much as possible. Provide personal warnings about upcoming transitions so the child can prepare. Move next to the child during transitions to provide modeling and support during the movement from one activity to another.
To recognize and be able to handle strong feelings	Read lots of stories and sing songs that explore feelings. Provide children with the vocabulary they need to identify a wide range of emotions. Look through magazines to find pictures of people expressing a variety of emotions. You can use these pictures to make puzzles and create collages. Make an emotions book with pictures of children in the class exhibiting the various emotions. Write stories about what might make children happy, sad, angry, scared, worried, excited, and so on.	Have materials in the classroom that children can use to identify feelings and express them safely (a punching pillow for anger, a hugging bear for sadness). Post pictures of people expressing a variety of feelings.	Help children identify feelings and redirect them into appropriate expressions of those feelings. Use words to acknowledge children's feelings and reassure them that the feelings are normal and that you will help them navigate the feelings. Allow for *all* emotions. Don't insist that children "put on a happy face" or "cheer up." Let children know that you care for them no matter what emotions they are experiencing. Model appropriate expression of emotions.
To have a sense of power and feel independent and competent	Provide pretend play opportunities in which children can take on roles of power. Plan open-ended experiences so children can choose how to use the materials. Provide ample free choice time so children can choose the areas in which they would like to play. Plan open-ended small-group activities that are in the zone of proximal development for the child. These activities take into account the child's developmental level and are planned to help him be successful with the guidance of an adult. Because the activities are open-ended, others can	Make materials accessible to children so they can select and use them independently. Post a job board and give children special jobs to do in the classroom. Provide materials at a variety of levels so children can be successful using them. Post panels that document children's learning and show what they did during various activities. Have children help create the panels and reflect on what they did during the activities.	Provide children with as many opportunities to make choices as possible. Help children fill out "I Did It!" cards to share with family members showing what children accomplished throughout the day. Acknowledge and describe what you notice the child doing well.

→

Figure 6.2 Strategies to Meet Children's Unmet Social and Emotional Needs (continued)

NEED	WAYS TO PROACTIVELY MEET THE NEED THROUGH . . .		
	Experiences	*Environments*	*Relationships*
To have a sense of power and feel independent and competent (continued)	also enjoy them even though they were planned for the child who is struggling. During small-group activities, refer children to each other for help based on what they can do well ("You can ask Fumio for help. I noticed he figured out how to get the paper to stick earlier.").		
To be engaged in stimulating pursuits	Plan experiences based on the HOMES principles of active learning (see chapter 2). Notice children's interests and plan learning experiences based on their interests and developmental levels. Focus more on small-group and individual interactions as opposed to large-group learning. Make sure children have plenty of opportunities to move throughout the day and during learning experiences.	Build environments around the HOMES principles of active learning (see chapter 2). Rotate materials in the classroom so there are always new and engaging materials to explore. Provide special materials to challenge and engage individual children, especially during difficult times, such as naps and diaper changings. Plan the daily routine so that most of the time is spent in free exploration of the classroom centers.	Interact with children while they are exploring, talk with them about how they are using materials, and provide additional materials to extend their engagement. Observe how children are using materials. Plan experiences and enhancements based on what you learn about children through these observations.
To enjoy relationships and have a sense of belonging	Sing songs that use children's names and incorporate their interests. Create many class books that incorporate children's ideas and interests. Help children work in different small groups and pairings to build multiple friendships. Plan collages or other art activities that involve all children's interests. Read stories about friendship and being a member of a community. Talk with children about what it means to be a good classmate.	Reflect children and their families in the classroom through pictures, books showing children that look like them, and music and pretend play materials that reflect their homes and cultures. Post photos of children and their families.	Greet each child and family. Express enthusiasm that they are part of the classroom community. At the end of each day, privately share with the child something you enjoyed about her during the day. Acknowledge when you see the child being a positive member of the classroom community, and specifically state what you see her doing.

Looking at This Approach in Action

There are many factors for teachers to consider when attempting to interpret a child's challenging behaviors based on social-emotional needs. Let's look at two examples that illustrate how teachers have used information about children's unmet needs to better support them in the classroom.

Jenae

Jenae is a four-year-old who has been in her current center for about two years. She moved up to the preK room a couple of months ago. The lead teacher, Ms. Oma, has been building a strong relationship with Jenae and her family since Jenae moved to the preK room. Two weeks ago, Jenae began to swear in the classroom. She is using inappropriate language at least three times a day and is directing it toward teachers and other children. In frustration, the teachers often send Jenae to the director's office in response to the swearing.

Through observations and conversations with Jenae's mom, Ms. Oma and her co-teachers have gathered information that might help them understand a little about Jenae's sudden habit of swearing. They notice that before swearing, Jenae often looks around as if assessing who might be paying attention to her. After swearing, she often laughs or smiles at the reactions she gets. Ms. Oma learns that Jenae's mom and dad have recently split up and that her dad has moved to another state. Jenae video chats with him periodically, but she has had very little contact with him since he left.

Jenae's mom has started a second job to make ends meet. When she picks Jenae up from school, they take two buses to her job as a medical transcriptionist. Jenae often sits by her mom's desk, watching cartoons on a tablet until she falls asleep. Her mom takes her home and puts her to bed late. Their day starts early the next morning, as Jenae is often dropped off at school as soon as it opens.

Based on her previous experience, Ms. Oma knows that swearing can cause chaos in the classroom, as other children react with shock or laughter and teachers are often taken aback at hearing the forbidden words. She also worries that Jenae is actually enjoying her time in the office and the special attention she receives from the director when she swears.

Putting all these clues together, Ms. Oma and her co-teachers conclude that Jenae's swearing is probably due to an unmet need for attention. They come up with a plan to give Jenae the attention she needs when she displays positive behaviors so that the swearing is no longer necessary.

First, every time Jenae swears, the teacher closest to her responds using the MoNSTeR response (see chapter 5). The teacher calmly moves close to Jenae, puts a hand on her shoulder, and with as little energy as possible says, "Please don't say that word." The teacher then redirects Jenae into an appropriate conversation. That teacher or another one says to the other children, who are often laughing or saying "Ooooohhhh," "Don't worry, we took care of it," and redirects their attention away from Jenae.

Meanwhile, the teachers look for other ways to fulfill Jenae's need for attention.

Experiences: Teachers look for ways to put Jenae in leadership roles during activities. They let her lead songs and movement exercises. They thank her for her leadership. During small groups, they draw attention to her successes. For example, "You worked so hard at that and you figured it out. Did you all see how Jenae got that big block to balance on the other one? That's pretty impressive."

They also use this technique to draw attention to times Jenae speaks appropriately in the classroom. Periodically, they draw other children's attention to something she says so that she receives affirmation for comments other than her swearing. For example, "Jenae, that was such a great story about what you were doing at the sand table just now. Hey guys, you should listen to this story! You will love it."

Environments: The teachers work with all children to create and post panels documenting their learning. During small-group experiences, they take pictures of children involved in the activities. The following day, they post the pictures along with applicable learning standards, a description of the experience, children's comments about what they did, and any artifacts (charts, children's stories, pictures) from the activity on a posterboard. They make sure to incorporate Jenae's comments in the panels. They encourage Jenae's mom to come into the classroom and spend a few minutes looking at and discussing the panels with her daughter.

Relationships: Ms. Oma works with Jenae's mom to find ways to build her relationship with Jenae. Her mom leaves little notes for Jenae that the teachers read to her during the day. They also help Jenae write letters to her dad.

Each teacher looks for ways to give Jenae one-on-one attention throughout the week. They no longer send Jenae to the office when she swears, but the director often pops in to see Jenae. At times, she will say, "I've heard that you are having a great day—that's awesome! Do you want to come and read a story with me in the office to celebrate?" All staff are finding ways to give Jenae the attention she needs during this difficult transition.

Teachers also enlist Jenae's mom in helping Jenae get the attention she needs. They provide her with talking points about the day's events at school so she can have conversations with her daughter during their long bus ride together. The teachers also give her simple games she can play with Jenae while on the bus or during quick breaks at her evening job.

Through these techniques, the adults in Jenae's life are feeding her need for attention in a variety of ways. At the same time, they are giving her as little attention as possible for swearing. Over time, as Jenae's need for attention is met consistently, the swearing disappears.

Daniel

Recently two-year-old Daniel has been acting aggressively toward other children. At least five times a day, teachers document that Daniel has hit, bit, or kicked another child, seemingly for no reason. Daniel is new to the program and was recently adopted by an older couple who brought him to his current center. He had been in foster care with the couple for a year before they adopted him. At first, Daniel's adoptive mother stayed home with him, but his parents eventually decided that time with other children would be good for him. Daniel is the couple's first child, and their home, although welcoming, is not designed for a curious toddler. Daniel has some toys in his room, but the rest of the house is off limits. Much of the furniture is light colored, and Daniel's mom is an avid collector of antique dolls, which are placed all over the house.

In school, teachers notice that Daniel tends to lash out at times when the children are transitioning between activities, such as diaper-changing or potty time, preparing for lunch, naptime, and when children are seated on the carpet waiting.

Based on all the information, the teachers determine that perhaps Daniel's need for stimulation is not being met. They come up with a plan to provide that stimulation.

Because the challenging behaviors occur primarily during transitions, Daniel's teachers focus their efforts on these times. First, they examine their daily routine to exclude as much waiting time and transitions as possible. For example, instead of having children wait during diaper-changing time, they stagger the changings so that one teacher can still engage with children while the other does changings and oversees potty time.

While getting ready for lunch, the teachers engage Daniel in helping set the tables. When his hands and mind are busy with a task, he is not looking for stimulation by messing with other children. Teachers also begin implementing family-style meals. Instead of giving children plates already filled with food, they place large bowls of food on the table. Teachers support children in serving themselves as soon as they have washed their hands and are seated at the table—as opposed to having to wait for all children to be seated—thus eliminating the waiting time and keeping children engaged in the meal prep process.

During naptime, teachers provide Daniel with a sensory toy he can hold and manipulate until he falls asleep. He tends to wake up early from his nap, so instead of giving him books or making him stay on his mat, teachers prepare a box with special materials that he uses only during this time. In the box, there are playdough and other toys that keep Daniel stimulated until the other children wake up.

Finally, the teachers work with Daniel's parents to create spaces in their home for him to be a toddler and play. They help the parents understand the developmental needs of a two-year-old and plan ways to provide outlets for

Daniel's need for stimulation. These include sending home various toys from school and planning outings at a local park so Daniel can burn off some energy.

Over time, Daniel's challenging behaviors decrease. Mondays continue to be difficult after he has been home over the weekend, but the teachers learn to anticipate his behaviors and intervene before he can strike out. While providing opportunities for Daniel's stimulation, the teachers also work to teach him the skills he needs to be successful in the classroom.

In both Jenae's and Daniel's scenarios, teachers were dedicated to supporting the children through their challenging behaviors. They recognized that through the challenging behaviors, Jenae and Daniel were expressing unmet social-emotional needs. By working to understand the behaviors and address the underlying needs instead of punishing the children, the teachers were able to reduce the behaviors. In doing so, they sent a powerful message to Jenae and Daniel and their families that the children were worth fighting for and that the world was not giving up on them because of their challenging behaviors—that Jenae and Daniel were more than their behaviors.

Important Points to Remember

Keep in mind several key points when dealing with behaviors that may reflect a child's unmet social and emotional needs:

Do not expect an immediate change in a child's behavior. If teachers are consistent with the approach, however, the behavior should start to decrease after a couple of weeks. The behavior might become more severe again after a weekend or some other break in the child's schedule, such as when a lead teacher is out for a couple of days or the child has a visit with the parent who does not have custody. But if the behavior shows no sign of decreasing within a couple of weeks, teachers may need to reevaluate their theory about the unmet need causing it and their approach to the situation.

The longer the need has been unmet, the longer it will take for the child to stop the behavior. If a child has been in and out of foster care since birth, for instance, it may take quite a long time for her to believe that she is loved and valued. It will take more intentional attention and time to build this sense in her so that she no longer needs to communicate her pain through the behavior.

The behavior may reemerge after it has been gone for a while. Often, an event in the child's life can trigger the reemergence of a challenging behavior, such as when his baby sibling is suddenly crawling and getting into his toys or his mom announces that she and her boyfriend are getting married. Or it may just be the child's inner insecurities resurfacing. In these instances, teachers can go back to the previous plan to address the behavior until it goes away again.

Open communication with families is essential during this process. If all adults in a child's life are focused on helping her build a sense of independence and competence, she will build that sense much more quickly and the challenging behavior will likely disappear before long.

Chapter Summary

Recognizing that children's unmet social and emotional needs can play a pivotal role in challenging behaviors allows teachers to view these behaviors through a lens of compassion as opposed to one of anger or frustration. As adults, we have the ability and the responsibility to let others know when our needs are not being met. However, young children cannot yet communicate this lack when they find themselves in the same situation. They have neither the language nor the self-knowledge to connect their behaviors with their inner turmoil. Instead, they let adults know that something is amiss through their behaviors. Just as the gardener carefully examines a plant and its environment to discover why the plant is not flourishing, the teacher must carefully observe a child and his environment to understand what the child is communicating through a behavior. Only then can the teacher come up with a plan to meet the child's needs, thereby making the challenging behavior unnecessary.

Chapter 7

Family Partnerships:
Build a Nurturing Community Garden

When children are exhibiting challenging behaviors, it takes a toll on both teachers and families. It can also increase tension between the two. Families sometimes feel like they are being blamed for their child's behavior and that teachers expect them to "fix" their child. Teachers sometimes feel like families blame them for the child's challenges and expect them to solve the problem immediately. Problem behaviors can strain relationships between families and teachers. However, when a child is consistently acting out, it is more important than ever that families and teachers work together for the benefit of the child and the classroom.

A strong partnership between families and teachers benefits children and classrooms at all times, but especially when a child is struggling with challenging behaviors. When teachers and families are on the same page and communicate regularly, they can come to a deeper understanding of what may be causing the behavior and what approaches might most benefit the child. The first step in establishing these partnerships is for teachers to build a spirit of collaboration with families, as opposed to one of blame and distrust. Teachers are experts in child development, and families are experts on their children. When each respects the knowledge of the other, the more they will see each other as valued partners.

Building relationships with families is an ongoing process. These strong relationships are important at all times and need to be developed and nurtured from the start. If the relationships are already established, it will make working together to address challenging behaviors that much easier. Like each child, each family is unique. To work effectively with a family, the early childhood teacher must get to know them. As author John Steinbeck wrote, "Try to understand men. If you understand each other, you will be kind to each other. Knowing a man well never leads to hate and almost always leads to love." The more a teacher knows about a child's family, the more effectively he can work with them to support the child.

A NOTE ON TERMS

Families come in all shapes and sizes. Some children live with one or both parents and some are being raised, either permanently or temporarily, by someone who is not a biological or adoptive parent. Others live with extended families who share caregiving duties. While this chapter tries to use the more inclusive terms *family* or *family members*, there are times when the simpler term *parent* is used. Please know that in this case, *parent* refers to anyone who has primary caregiving responsibilities for the child.

Strategies for Building Relationships with Families

The following strategies can help teachers build relationships with families:

Ask open-ended questions. Saying to a family, "Tell me about mealtimes in your home," or asking, "What special days do you celebrate in your family?" helps a teacher understand a child's life at home. This understanding can help the teacher support the child in the classroom, connect with the family, and incorporate aspects of the child's home life into the classroom. Asking questions about differences in a respectful way is not intrusive or rude. Instead, ignoring differences can send the message that they are taboo and not to be discussed.

Make connections. Teachers can look for ways to build connections with family members. For example, "I noticed that your family does not eat meat. I am trying to eat more vegetarian meals myself. Maybe you can give me some recipes to try?" Or, "Josiah said you all love to dance to the Black Eyed Peas. That sounds like so much fun. I love that band." When teachers make and build on these connections, they plant the seeds for strong family partnerships.

Use a family survey. A more formal way to build connections is to create a survey for new families. Along with giving teachers information about families, a survey also helps families feel welcome and special as teachers show interest in them. Teachers can use the information to help children integrate into the classroom, reflect a family's culture in the space, and find common connections with families. Refer to the "Getting to Know You: A Family Survey" form on pages 170–171 in the appendix.

Suspend judgment. Did you know that around 70 percent of Americans make their beds each morning and the rest do not? Each of us grew up in, and are part of, a family that had its own traditions and ways of doing things, like having to make your bed in the morning. While these traditions may feel familiar, that does not make them "right." Eating dinner in front of the TV is not "wrong" or "right." Some families do it, and some do not. When a teacher can approach each family with a spirit of openness, respect, and learning, she is better able to build strong relationships with them.

As teachers get to know children's families, they will come to understand them—especially their desires and dreams for their children. This understanding will help teachers build solid partnerships with parents, which are sure to benefit children.

A NOTE ON SAFETY

While it is important to suspend judgment and seek to understand and value each family, it is our first priority that children be safe and in homes that provide for their physical and emotional needs. Above all, as early childhood providers, we must prioritize children's well-being and remember that we are mandated reporters. This means that if we have concerns that a child is not safe or that his home is not healthy, we are mandated by law to report those concerns to the management at our school or center and to applicable state agencies. It is not the duty of teachers to investigate or prove their concerns: It is only their duty to report them. We want to build meaningful partnerships with families, but that goal comes second to keeping children safe and healthy.

Communicating with Families About Challenging Behavior

When there is already a strong relationship in place, the topic of challenging behavior is easier to broach. Families are less likely to ignore the issue or express defensiveness. The goal of the communication should be to share information and to work together to address the issue, not to punish or discipline the child for behaviors that occur in the classroom. Young children are not able to connect their actions during the school day with consequences given at home. Once children are older and in elementary school, this may change. But in the early childhood years, there is very little parents can do at home that will impact their child's behavior at school. When teachers communicate about challenging behaviors, the message should be, "This happened, and we handled it at school in this way. I wanted you to know in case your child mentions it."

Another reason families cannot have much effect on children's classroom behavior is because the behavior may not occur at home. Many of the situations that cause challenging behaviors in school do not exist at home, such as having to share materials all the time, having to stand in line, and frequently transitioning from one activity to another. Likewise, families usually do not have the same social and behavioral expectations for children at home as teachers do at school. And, as discussed in chapter 1, these expectations are often at the root of challenging behaviors. If children do not display the problem behaviors at home, families do not have the opportunity to address them. The best parents can do is support the school's efforts and keep the lines of communication open.

If the behavior does occur at home, teachers and families can agree to address it in the same way. This might mean using the same techniques to teach the social skills children need, making the same revisions to children's environments, or using the same words to relate behavioral expectations. If families and teachers determine that a child's behavior is the result of an unmet social-emotional need, they can work together to come up with a plan to meet the child's need so that the behavior is no longer necessary.

Family Check-In Conferences

It is important to keep the lines of communication open while dealing with challenging behaviors. Having planned check-in conferences along with the regular family-teacher conferences allows teachers and families to share information and develop a plan for dealing with the behavior so that it is consistently addressed by the adults in a child's life. These conferences are essential in building a spirit of collaboration with families, so teachers need to look for ways to establish this spirit when planning and conducting the conferences. Naturally, the thought of conferences about problem behaviors can be stressful for teachers and families. The following tips can help make them effective relationship-building tools to benefit the child.

Tips for Effective Family Conferences

Assume shared goals. Both the teacher and the parent want what is best for the child. They may have different ideas of what "best" looks like, but both are committed to helping the child. The conference will go better if both teacher and parent enter it believing that they share the same goal and that they can find ways to work together to support the child through this challenging period.

Use language of collaboration. Teachers need to be aware of what their nonverbal communication is saying to the parent. For instance, the environment will feel more collaborative if teachers sit next to, and not across from, the parent. Teachers can also hold their arms open instead of crossed to set a more positive and open tone. Relaxed body language signals that teachers are ready to work together with the family on behalf of the child. In verbal communications, teachers build collaboration by using words like *we* and *together*. Conversations are more likely to be productive when teachers keep the focus on the child and express confidence that, together, the teacher and family can find a solution for the issue at hand.

Open with an anecdote. Most families enjoy hearing stories about their children. Starting the conference with an endearing story about something their child did in the classroom breaks the ice and cuts the tension. It also helps families understand that the teacher is not only focused on the negative and that positive behaviors also happen in the classroom. Teachers can avoid terms like *normal* and *bad* and other words that might cause families to feel like their child is under attack.

Present the documentation without judgment. Let the documentation of the child's behavior speak for itself. (See the "Behavior Documentation Form" in the appendix on page 168.) There is no need for teachers to add their personal judgments. Typically, families will already feel bad about the behavior and will be worried about what it means for their child. If the teacher focuses on the behavior itself instead of passing judgment on it, the family may be less likely to get defensive or put up walls of resistance. When the documentation is well done, families will see the issue without the teacher having to articulate it.

Listen. At every conference, families should get as much time to speak as the teacher has. Families need the opportunity to share what they notice about their child, and teachers need to actively listen and try to hear what families are saying. What concerns do they have? The conference should also include opportunities for caregivers to ask their questions and receive answers.

Discuss goals and problem-solve. The bulk of the conference should be dedicated to teachers and families working together to discuss goals and develop a plan to meet those goals. Together, parents and teachers can decide on two or three behavioral goals for the child. These goals should be specific and realistic and directly related to the behavior in question. After the goals are established, families and teachers can develop a plan to support the child in successfully meeting those goals. A plan might include establishing ways to meet unmet social-emotional needs, both at home and at school. It might also include deciding on consistent language and reactions that both parties will use when the behavior occurs.

Provide resources for support. At times, there may be community agencies, helpful reading, or other resources that might be of help to families as they face the reality of having a child with challenging behaviors. Teachers can share these resources with parents during the conference.

Make a plan for follow-up. Before ending the conference, families and teachers should make a plan for follow-up. This includes agreeing on how they will continue to communicate, setting a date for the next check-in conference, and assigning any actions either party will do. Part of a plan might also be scheduling a time for the parent to observe the child in the classroom so she can gain a better understanding of her child's behavior.

Express appreciation and confidence. Conferences should end on a positive note, with teachers thanking the family for their time and dedication to the process and for sharing their child with the center. Teachers can also reiterate to families their confidence that together they can help the child navigate this difficult period.

Well-planned and collaborative family conferences are essential to the process of supporting a child through these trying times. Children reap the benefit when the adults in their lives work together. Ongoing communication with families—both formal (conferences) and informal (conversations at drop-off and pickup times)—is an important component of a collaborative working relationship.

Addressing Conflicts Between Teachers and Families

For most parents, their child is the most valuable person in their lives. It can be very emotional for them to leave their child in the care of another adult. These emotions may become even more heightened when parents hear that their child is struggling. Conflicts may arise between teachers and families as they both strive to find answers for how to help the child. Even when teachers put their best foot forward, families may still react negatively simply because they are upset about a situation and are looking for someone to blame. In some cases, parents' behaviors reflect their feelings about their own less-than-ideal school experiences, their deep concern that they are being judged, or cultural differences around what children need.

When conflicts with families arise, teachers can improve the chances of reaching an effective solution by using a conflict resolution model similar to the one laid out for children in chapter 4. By using the following five steps during the conference, teachers can involve families in resolving the conflict and reaching an agreeable solution.

The Five Steps of Conflict Resolution in Family Conferences

Step 1: State the conflict. The first step in the conflict resolution process is to state the conflict so that the teacher and the family both understand the issue. For example, a teacher might begin by saying, "You would like us to start the toilet training process with Vinnie. I am concerned that he is not yet ready for this step. We are here to see how we can work together to support him."

Step 2: Brainstorm solutions. The second step is to work together to brainstorm possible solutions. In the brainstorming process, there are no right or wrong answers. The brainstorming starts with an open-ended question, such as, "What would you like to see happen in this situation?"

Step 3: Evaluate and choose from solutions. After listing the solutions, teachers and families evaluate each one by considering its pros and cons. Together they pick a solution that will work best for all three parties: the family, the teacher, and, most importantly, the child.

Step 4: Restate the chosen solution. Restate the solution so everyone is clear on it. For example, the teacher might say, "Over the next four weeks, I am going to observe Vinnie for signs of toilet readiness. I will use this checklist on toilet readiness. At home, you will put out a potty chair and see if Vinnie shows interest. We will read the story about toilet use with him once or twice over the next month."

Step 5: Plan for follow-up. Once all parties are in agreement, the conference should conclude with a plan to follow up. The teacher might end by saying, "Thank you so much for taking the time to work on a solution with me. I know that we are both committed to doing the best for Vinnie. Let's touch base in two weeks to make sure we are both still following our plan."

Addressing conflicts is no one's favorite part of being an early childhood professional. But when teachers and families are dealing with something as important as a child's well-being, conflicts may occur. Telling a family that their child is struggling with challenging behaviors is very difficult—*almost* as difficult as it is to be the parent hearing that news. How teachers address these conflicts can help families know that they and teachers are both focused on what is best for the child. This knowledge can go a long way in building strong relationships with families, and these relationships are the cornerstone of a supportive classroom environment in which all children thrive and in which those who are struggling have a greater chance at success.

It is important that all parties leave a conference with a clear understanding of what was discussed and of any plans to moving forward. It helps to document these discussions on a form, such as the "Family-Teacher Conference Form" on pages 172–173 of the appendix.

Chapter Summary

Plants fare better when gardeners pool their knowledge and work together to ensure plants' success. In the same way, children benefit greatly when the adults in their lives come together to work for their success in the classroom. The early childhood professional brings to the table an understanding of child development and experience working with children. A child's family members contribute knowledge of the unique needs of their child. When both parties commit to a partnership, they are more likely to find solutions that benefit the child's experience in the classroom as well as at home.

Chapter 8

A Comprehensive Approach to Challenging Behaviors:
Help All Seedlings Thrive

In this book, we have looked at many approaches to addressing challenging behaviors in the classroom. Some of these strategies are proactive—they create a classroom environment, both the physical and the social-emotional space, in which challenging behaviors are less likely to occur. And some strategies are reactive, or supportive—they include specific steps teachers can take in response to challenging behaviors once they occur. Addressing challenging behavior is like peeling an onion. A teacher dedicated to helping all children thrive (as opposed to "fixing" a single child) must peel back the layers, one by one, as she looks for the cause of problem behaviors so she can give children the tools needed for success.

Let's use our gardening analogy to look at how all these strategies come together in one comprehensive eight-step approach, spelled out in **figure 8.1** on pages 134–135. Then, we'll examine each of the steps in more detail. These steps may not flow in a perfect sequence, one after another, but they provide a framework for how to understand, respond to, and help resolve challenging behaviors. We will also look at a scenario involving a student in Ms. Noemi's class and how she follows the steps to address the challenging behavior.

Figure 8.1 A Comprehensive Eight-Step Approach to Challenging Behaviors

PROACTIVE STRATEGIES TO PREVENT AND REDUCE CHALLENGING BEHAVIORS

Gardener's Role	Teacher's Role	Explanation of Steps
Before planting season even begins, the gardener prepares the soil so plants are more likely to be successful.	To ensure that most children thrive, the teacher proactively creates a classroom designed around what children need and how they learn.	**Step 1: Create a classroom around children's needs.** When classroom environments are built around how children learn, children are less likely to exhibit challenging behaviors in the face of inappropriate expectations. (See chapter 1 and the "Classroom Factors Observation Form" on pages 163–164.)
		Step 2: Incorporate active learning. When teachers incorporate the tenets of active learning into how they plan their lessons and design their environments, they are teaching how children learn. (See chapter 2 and the "HOMES Active Learning Scale" on page 162.)
		Step 3: Build relationships with children. Teachers use what they know about children's development and build relationships with individual children in their care to create optimal growing conditions. (See chapter 3.)

SUPPORTIVE STRATEGIES TO RESPOND TO CHALLENGING BEHAVIORS

Gardener's Role	Teacher's Role	Explanation of Steps
As plants grow, the gardener observes the conditions to make sure the environment is allowing for optimal growth and development, paying close attention to those plants that may not be thriving.	If a child appears to struggle in the classroom (exhibit challenging behaviors), the teacher documents the struggle and observes the classroom environment to look for clues as to what might be causing the behaviors.	**Step 4: Observe and document the child's behavior.** The teacher's first step is to begin a process of observation and documentation to discover the conditions that can be addressed to positively impact the child's experience. These observations should focus on what classroom factors might be contributing to the challenging behaviors. You can use the "Classroom Factors Observation Form" (pages 163–164) and the "Behavior Documentation Form" (page 168) to help with this process. These forms help teachers spot patterns or other clues as to what factors may be contributing to the child's behavior. (See chapters 1 and 2 and the filled-out sample forms in **figures 8.2 and 8.3** on pages 145 and 146–148.)
After observing the growing conditions, the gardener makes tweaks to the environment to remove impediments to a plant's growth.	A teacher uses information gained through observation to remedy classroom factors that may be causing a child's behavior. Often, while the classroom adaptation is in response to one child's behavior, the resulting change benefits all children.	**Step 5: Address environmental factors affecting the child.** Once the teacher has identified what may be causing some of the challenging behaviors, she can make changes in the environment to help the child be more successful. This may mean changing expectations for the child, adapting the physical environment, or adjusting the classroom routine. These changes may stop the behavior by eliminating the conditions that lead to it. If the behavior persists, the teacher keeps looking for strategies to support the child's success in the classroom. (See chapters 1–4.)
At times, a plant might need additional supports. The gardener looks for and uses supportive tools with a plant that needs guidance (for example, stakes for sunflowers and cages for tomatoes).	At times, children may continue to struggle in the classroom even after the teacher adjusts the environment. The teacher looks for and implements strategies that support these children in meeting the social and behavioral demands of the classroom.	**Step 6: Help the child learn social skills.** Teachers focus their efforts on strategies that help children learn and meet the social expectations of the classroom. These strategies are designed to help children learn, as opposed to punishing them for misbehaviors that are, in reality, an indication of a lack of understanding of or ability to meet classroom expectations. (See chapter 4.)

Gardener's Role	Teacher's Role	Explanation of Steps
The gardener knows there is great power in collective knowledge. She seeks out the support of others as she plans for and supports the crops in her garden.	Children can only benefit when the most important adults in their lives (their parents and teachers) come together to share knowledge and find ways to support their experiences in the classroom. As these adults collaborate, they also model mutually respectful partnerships for children.	**Step 7: Hold a family conference.** When children struggle with challenging behaviors, both teachers and family members have knowledge that can affect a child's success in the classroom. A family conference provides a formal time for family adults to meet with teachers to make a plan for a child. Provide time in the conference for everyone to share observations, celebrate the child's strengths, discuss concerns, and decide together on strategies and goals for the child. When a child is struggling, these conferences should be held regularly to keep the lines of communication open. (See chapter 7 and **figure 8.4** on page 149 as well as "Getting to Know You: A Family Survey" on pages 170–171 and the "Family-Teacher Conference Form" on pages 172–173.)
If the plant continues to struggle, the gardener looks for further ways to meet its unmet needs. This might include moving the plant to a more or less shady location, repotting the plant, or applying a special fertilizer.	If a child continues to struggle, the teacher implements a plan to identify the social-emotional needs that may be unmet and strategies to meet these needs—thus eliminating the child's need for the behavior.	**Step 8: Plan to meet the child's unmet social and emotional needs.** For some children, unmet social-emotional needs are at the root of their challenging behaviors. The situation may be due to a recent disruption (a new baby in the house, a divorce, or a parent being deployed) or more long-term (in and out of foster care, death of a parent, abuse). When the teacher identifies the need, often with the help of the family, she can make a plan to meet this need through classroom activities, interactions, and learning spaces. (See chapters 6 and 7 and **figure 8.5** on page 150 as well as the blank form on page 174 of the appendix.)

Proactive Strategies to Prevent and Reduce Challenging Behaviors

Children are more likely to be successful in an environment that is built around their developmental needs and how they learn. When teachers proactively incorporate developmentally appropriate spaces, active learning, and relationship-building strategies, children are more likely to be able to effectively navigate the classroom environment.

Step 1: Create a Classroom Around Children's Needs

First, teachers plan spaces meant to engage children's senses and provide developmentally appropriate expectations. They look at the classroom through the eyes of the children and seek to incorporate items that are interesting to see, hear, smell, and touch. You can use the "Classroom Factors Observation Form" on pages 163–164 of the appendix to help with this process. When teachers build classrooms in this way, they are proactively creating spaces that lessen the possibility that children will act out against inappropriate expectations with challenging behaviors.

Step 2: Incorporate Active Learning

Active learning classrooms are those in which teachers plan to meet the true long-term learning needs of children by building experiences and learning environments around the HOMES model. See page 162 for a blank form you can use to score classroom activities and experiences. Teachers plan activities that are *hands-on*, in which children use and interact with real and interesting materials. The experiences are also *open-ended*. Teachers provide materials and allow children to use the materials however they choose, expanding their learning through conversations and questions. Teachers also build experiences around topics that are *meaningful* for children and based on their interests instead of on a preset calendar of themes or topics. Teachers *engage* children's brains through interactions, asking them interesting questions instead of ones they already know the answers to, and by planning *sensory-oriented* learning experiences as opposed to rote learning based on memorization.

Step 3: Build Relationships with Children

Finally, teachers proactively prepare classrooms for children's success when they build solid relationships with children and their families. When teachers truly know and appreciate children as individuals, they can better plan around children's developmental needs and interests. When children feel known and valued, they develop stronger senses of self and community. These feelings provide a foundation for a learning environment in which children feel successful and have no need to communicate using challenging behaviors.

Ms. Noemi is a teacher in a preK classroom. Like many teachers, she struggles with challenging behaviors. Lately, her classroom seems chaotic. The first six weeks of school went smoothly, but now she is struggling to get children to settle down and pay attention during group time and to follow directions at other times of day. At a training session, Ms. Noemi learns about proactively building classrooms around how children learn, instead of trying to get children to learn the way she is used to teaching. Ms. Noemi looks at the factors in her classroom that may be contributing to challenging behaviors and records her observations. She then makes the following changes to her classroom and teaching routine:

She makes her circle times more engaging. She incorporates opportunities for children to move and be actively involved. She eliminates the routines of calendar time and having children recite the alphabet every morning after realizing that these daily drills are not helping children learn and that they are causing children to be bored and act out. She also removes the requirement that children sit crisscross applesauce and allows them to sit comfortably during this time of day, telling them that as long as they don't bother anyone, they can attend however it makes sense for them. Some children sit, others lie down, and some stand. Some children even walk around. She finds that by lessening her control, children behave better.

She eliminates "art time" from her daily routine and increases children's free choice time. Ms. Noemi recognizes that many children were exhibiting challenging behaviors during this time of the daily routine. She realizes that these behaviors were most likely in response to her focus on getting children to follow directions instead of letting them express themselves through their art. Instead of having art be time of day, she enhances her art center and encourages children to use the materials as they wish during free choice time. She often sits with them and asks about the choices they make, how they are using the materials, and their creations. She is amazed at the interesting work children produce when given the freedom to do so. She also finds that giving children autonomy in how they spend their time and use materials results in fewer challenging behaviors.

She makes some changes to how she transitions children from one activity to another. Previously Ms. Noemi spent a lot of time and energy trying to get children to stand in a straight line with their hands at their sides and "holding a bubble" (see page 83) in their mouths. Often, minutes went by as the class waited for everyone to comply with her behavioral expectations. Even children who did not typically struggle with challenging behaviors lost patience and left the line or started poking or bothering others. Some started to fuss and cry as they anticipated going outside and did not understand why the transition was taking so long. Now, Ms. Noemi simply gathers the children together, counts them, and finds a fun way to move with them to the next activity. This might include singing a silly song, hopping like bunnies, or moving like a train. Challenging behaviors are no longer an issue during these transitions, since Ms. Noemi's expectations are now more appropriate for the children's developmental levels.

Finally, she puts more intentional focus on building relationships with the children in her class. She creates a chart with each child's name. Over the course of a week, she makes a mark next to children's names as she spends one-on-one time with each child. She makes it a goal to ensure that each child gets at least three marks over the course of two weeks. During these interactions, she focuses on engaging in real conversations with children about what they are doing, their lives, and their interests. Whenever possible, she incorporates elements into the classroom based on what she learns in these conversations. For example, after talking with one child about his interest in making costumes, Ms. Noemi collects fabric scraps from families and incorporates them into the classroom.

All these proactive changes make a big difference in Ms. Noemi's classroom. Children appear more engaged and interested in classroom experiences, and incidents of challenging behaviors are greatly reduced. Ms. Noemi also finds that she enjoys her job much more now that she doesn't have to fight as much to control the children.

Supportive Strategies to Respond to Challenging Behaviors

As teachers create more-supportive and appropriate learning environments, challenging behaviors will decrease. When more children are engaged with materials and in activities designed to meet their learning needs, their behaviors will communicate this. A calmer environment will also tend to highlight children who may need more-targeted supports.

> While most children are much calmer and display fewer challenging behaviors following Ms. Noemi's changes to the classroom and routines, one child, Ashley, continues to struggle. Ashley's challenges become even more evident as the rest of the children appear to have an easier time.
>
> Recently, Ashley's outbursts have been a problem in the classroom. After two or three incidents, Ms. Noemi begins a documentation process.

Step 4: Observe and Document the Child's Behaviors

Once a child exhibits a behavior more than once or twice, a teacher needs to begin to document information about the behavior to gain a deeper understanding of what might be causing it. Through this observation, the teacher gathers information about what leads to the behavior and what emotions and thoughts the child appears to express while engaging in it. The purpose of this observation is to formulate a plan for how to best help the child successfully navigate the classroom community.

For documentation to be most helpful, it must be objective and based on the facts of the situation. These facts include what happened, who was there, and what was said. A teacher's interpretations of and feelings about the behavior should not be part of this description. Through her observations, a teacher paints a picture that allows others to understand the situation and draw their own conclusions based on the facts presented. After recounting the facts, a teacher can document more subjective information on an observation form, which can serve to clarify what a child might be communicating through the behavior. This information might include what a child appears to be feeling and what conclusions a teacher draws based on the observations. See the sample forms in figure 8.3 on pages 146–148 and the blank "Behavior Documentation Form" on page 168 of the appendix.

The goal of documentation is to allow teachers to look for patterns and possible motivations behind the child's behavior. Clear, concise, and fact-based observations can provide the information needed for teachers to identify the factors contributing to the behaviors and make good decisions for how to respond.

Over a couple of weeks, Ms. Noemi and her co-teacher, Mr. Jamal, document any behavior incidents involving Ashley. They are careful to stay close to Ashley as much as possible so they can respond quickly, and they also try to determine what led to each incident so they can understand what may be causing the behavior. See step 5 for some examples of the documentation they gathered. Using these notes, the teachers identify some factors that may be contributing to Ashley's behaviors.

Step 5: Address Environmental Factors Affecting the Child

As teachers review documentation, the first goal should be to look for clues about classroom factors that may be contributing to the challenging behavior. For example:

Does the behavior usually occur in the same area of the classroom? There might be something about the area that is not working for the child. Maybe it is too small, or there are not enough materials, or the child does not understand how to use the materials or how to interact with others in the center. Making some changes to the area in question may reduce the behavior.

Does the behavior happen around the same time of day? It could be that the child has a physical issue that contributes to the behavior at that time of day. For example, if challenging behaviors happen in late morning, the child might be hungry and unable to communicate it. If the behavior happens during naptime, the child might not be tired and the expectation of having to stay on a cot and be quiet for an hour is too much for him to handle. Finally, if the behavior always occurs toward the end of the day, it could be that the stress of being in a group setting all day and having to conform to classroom rules and expectations becomes too much for him by this time. By adjusting the child's schedule, making different provisions for his physical needs, and making other arrangements for him during challenging parts of the day, a teacher can help the child be more successful in the classroom. See "Strategies for Addressing Challenging Behaviors Throughout the Day" on pages 165–167 of the appendix for proactive and supportive strategies to help children during challenging times of day.

Does the behavior happen during similar classroom segments? For example, the behavior may occur during transition times or when children are in a large group. This information could inspire a teacher to shift the expectations for that time of day for the child. For example, maybe the child should not be expected to participate in circle time or needs to be able to walk around while participating. If transitions are challenging, teachers can make special arrangements to support the child through them.

Documentation is an essential piece of the puzzle of challenging behavior. Thorough documentation can provide teachers with an extensive record of the behavior that they can look back at when they are not dealing with the behavior and the stress that comes with it. Once teachers are separated by time and space from the behavior, they may be able to see patterns and clues emerge from the documentation. When a teacher has identified the issues, she can take steps to remedy the classroom factors that may be contributing to the behavior in question.

At times, it may be difficult for teachers to objectively look at their classrooms to see how some factors may be motivating challenging behaviors. It can be very helpful to invite another member of the center community to conduct an observation focused on these factors. Another set of eyes can be crucial in looking at ways to adapt the classroom environment so a child can be more successful. The "Classroom Factors Observation Form" on pages 163–164 of the appendix can be used for this purpose.

Ms. Noemi, Mr. Jamal, and their director Maya sit down to look at the documentation together. They identify two factors that they can revise to help Ashley be more successful in the classroom. The first is an adaptation to the block center. They notice that many of Ashley's outbursts started because of situations in the block center. Upon reflection, they realize that the block center has been especially popular lately. Based on their observations, they decide to expand the block center to accommodate more children at a time. They move shelves to make the library smaller and plan to start hosting group experiences in the block center instead of the library.

The next adjustment the teachers make is in regards to expectations for Ashley. Her behavior indicates that storytime is especially challenging for her. When she is bored, she bothers the children around her. They decide on a few strategies to help Ashley navigate this time of day. While storytime is always optional, they decide to be more intentional in telling Ashley this. Before every storytime, Mr. Jamal will say to Ashley, "We are going to read a story now. Would you like to sit with me and listen or find something else quiet to do in the classroom?" If she chooses to participate, Mr. Jamal will sit with her to help her be successful. If she does not, he will help her settle into another quiet activity before joining the group himself for storytime. They also decide to give Ashley a toy to hold in her hands during any group experience she is part of. This will ensure that her hands are busy during these times so she is less likely to touch other children.

The teachers and director are confident that through these simple revisions, they are making the classroom more conducive to Ashley's needs, thus making it less likely that she will exhibit challenging behaviors.

Step 6: Help the Child Learn Social Skills

At times, the documentation may indicate that a child needs help learning the social skills required to get along in the classroom. For example:

The behavior occurs when the child is waiting with nothing to occupy his time and mind. Examples include times when children have washed their hands and are waiting for meals, when they are sitting at tables waiting for small-group time to start, when they are lined up to go outside, or when they are waiting for their turn in the bathroom. In these cases, the teacher might take a two-pronged approach: He can look for ways to lessen wait times in the classroom and also look for ways to work with the child to develop the ability to wait when necessary.

The behavior occurs because the child does not know how to enter social situations. The child may want to join the play of other children or see a child playing with a material that looks interesting. In this case, the teacher can identify those situations before they happen and intervene to help the child join the play. The teacher can assist the child in developing the skills needed to develop and maintain social relationships.

The behavior appears when the child is faced with frustration. Again, the teacher can use this information to plan a two-pronged approach: she can look for ways to limit the factors that cause frustration and she can work with the child to build competence in dealing with frustration.

In any of these cases, the documentation may help a teacher understand that the child's challenging behavior is a result of him not understanding or not yet having the skills to comply with classroom expectations. When teachers are in the midst of teaching, balancing the needs of many children, and addressing challenging behaviors simultaneously, it can be difficult to see what might be causing a child's distress. The child's behavioral patterns may only become obvious as teachers review the documentation. Once a teacher understands that a child needs additional support to develop social skills, she can implement a plan to guide this process.

In reviewing the documentation, Ashley's teachers also recognize the opportunity to help her deal with frustration in social situations. Through close observation, they recognize that, when she is frustrated, Ashley usually screams or makes some other verbalization before striking out. Ms. Noemi and Mr. Jamal come up with a plan to help give Ashley the tools to deal with this strong emotion and be successful in the classroom setting.

The teachers will rotate days. On her or his day, the assigned teacher will be especially observant of Ashley's interactions. Upon witnessing her frustration, the teacher will hurry to Ashley's side and interrupt the situation. The teacher will touch Ashley in a reassuring way, physically separate Ashley and the source of her frustration, and affirm her emotions by saying something like, "It is so hard when things don't happen the way you want." Based on the situation, the teacher will give Ashley two choices for what to do. For example, "Your blocks fell. That is frustrating. Do you want me to help you rebuild your structure, or should we go run in place in the movement area for a few minutes to burn off some steam?"

After a couple of weeks of these interventions, the teachers notice that Ashley's behavior improves. They are thrilled when one day a child trips and falls into Ashley and, instead of striking out, Ashley stomps her foot, turns away, and begins to run in place.

However, after reading through more documentation, Ms. Noemi and Mr. Jamal find that Ashley has picked up a new behavior—she has started swearing. Based on this new behavior, the teachers decide to call a family conference.

Step 7: Hold a Family Conference

Supporting a child with challenging behaviors can be trying for all those involved. The process will go much smoother if teachers and families work together for the benefit of the child. When a behavior grows frequent enough that teachers are compiling documentation, teachers and family members should plan a time to meet to discuss the child and how best to help him succeed in the classroom environment.

The purpose of this conference is for the teacher and family members to share their experiences of the child's behavior, discuss the possible purposes of the behavior, and develop a coordinated plan for addressing it. See the "Family-Teacher Conference Form" on pages 172–173 of the appendix. At times, the presence of challenging behaviors can cause tension between teachers and families. Parents may feel like teachers are blaming them for their child's behaviors. Teachers may feel like parents are not listening or are not concerned about the situation. Open and honest communication can help avoid this tension and lead to partnerships that benefit the child. For more information about conducting conferences and partnering with families, see chapter 7.

During a family conference, teachers and family members should plan regular check-ins to touch base on the child's progress and to review and revise the behavior plan as needed. When families and teachers work as a team, it benefits all children, especially a child who is struggling with challenging behaviors.

Ms. Noemi and her director Maya decide to arrange a family conference with Ashley's mom, dad, and stepdad. They planned to schedule it early in the morning before Ashley's parents go to work. Her mom and stepdad could make it early, but her dad's schedule was trickier. They tried to arrange for Ashley's dad to join via video conference, but because of the time change, he was unable to attend. Instead, they agreed that Ashley's mom would convey the information to the dad and that Maya would make herself available by phone if Ashley's dad had any follow-up questions or comments.

Ms. Noemi starts the conference by talking about Ashley's strengths and assuring her parents that this conference is about working together to help Ashley be successful in the classroom, as opposed to complaining about her and insisting that the family find a solution. Ms. Noemi also asks Ashley's parents to reflect on their daughter's strengths at home, and she writes their ideas on the conference form.

Next, Ms. Noemi and Maya share their documentation with the parents and talk about Ashley's swearing. Her mother shares that she and Ashley's stepdad are also starting to see some of this behavior at home. Besides having a new baby in the house, Ashley's father moved across the country a few months earlier, and she has not seen him in person in a long time. Ashley's mom worries that all of this may be contributing to the behavior. Maya assures Ashley's mom that, while the behavior is not what they want to see, they have seen it before and are sure that they can help Ashley get through it.

Based on the documentation and what they know about Ashley, the adults conclude that with all the transition in Ashley's life, she may feel she is not getting enough attention. As a result of the meeting, they come up with a plan to give as little attention as possible to Ashley when she swears and to find proactive ways to get her the positive attention she craves so that she no longer needs to use swearing to communicate.

Step 8: Plan to Meet the Child's Unmet Social and Emotional Needs

Most of the time, children's behaviors are communicating that they are struggling with some aspect of the classroom environment, whether that be a classroom factor that is a mismatch for the child or that the child lacks the needed social skills to be successful. By changing their expectations and offering patient instruction, caring teachers can guide children through their difficulties. At times, however, children struggle even in the most responsive of classrooms. These cases often suggest that a child's behavior is driven by an unmet social-emotional need.

If the challenging behavior is not responding to classroom adaptations or methods that teach social skills, it is time for the child's teachers and families (whenever possible) to determine which unmet need may be at the root of the behavior and develop a plan to meet that need. (See page 169 of the appendix for a list of children's social-emotional needs.) This process requires the teacher to reflect both on the documentation of the behavior and on what she knows about the child and his life outside of the classroom. Teachers can use the "Plan to Meet Child's Social and Emotional Needs" form on page 174 to guide their reflections and document their thoughts on how they might address the unmet need through the environments they create, the interactions they plan, and the relationships they build with children.

The adults in Ashley's life conclude that her swearing is a result of her need for attention not being met. They come up with a plan to give Ashley plenty of extra attention over the next few weeks so that she no longer needs to swear. Ms. Noemi, Mr. Jamal, Maya, and the rest of the center staff will find ways to give attention to Ashley when she is in the classroom. Meanwhile, Ashley's mom and stepdad, along with her dad via video call, will assure Ashley that she is an important part of their family when she is at home. The adults in her life also find ways to build solid familial bonds while Ashley is at school. See figures 8.4 and 8.5 on pages 149–150 for some ideas as to how the adults in Ashley's life will meet her need for attention in the environments they create, the activities they plan, and how they interact with Ashley.

Because all the adults in her life are focused on her success, their interventions begin to show results within a couple of weeks, with Ashley only swearing a couple of times. The adults notice that she is more likely to swear after a video call with her dad, so they help Ashley find healthy ways to express her feelings about her dad's absence.

Within six weeks, the swearing is completely gone. Ashley is back to being the bubbly and determined girl they all knew before her troubling behavior began. Along with getting the positive attention she needs, Ashley is gaining skills to deal with the strong emotions she's experiencing. Because her teachers were focused on helping her be successful, as opposed to punishing or changing her, Ashley continues to be a valued member of Ms. Noemi and Mr. Jamal's classroom community.

Chapter Summary

The proficient gardener is methodical in how she approaches the development of the plants she sows, from the preparation of the soil to the day-to-day care she takes in meeting the unique needs of each seedling. When a plant fails to thrive, she looks for ways to help it succeed. The eight steps discussed in this chapter outline a similar approach for teachers—one that is rooted in the belief that each child can be successful, given the right environment. When teachers view every child through this lens of potential, children are more likely to see themselves in that same light.

Ashley's teachers, while frustrated with her behavior, recognized that it was communicating something and that their job was to decipher the message so they could remedy the situation causing the behavior. Like gardeners, Ashley's teachers were committed to adapting their practices and classroom environments so she could find her way to success.

Figure 8.2 Sample Classroom Factors Observation Form:
Ms. Noemi's Classroom

Classroom: PreK—2   **Teacher:** Ms. Noemi   **Date(s):** November 2—5

CLASSROOM FACTOR		CLASSROOM EXAMPLE	OBSERVATION NOTES
Appropriateness of Expectations	Too high expectations for self-control	Teacher expects that children stand in a straight line before they go outside.	Many children do not pay attention during circle time. They seem bored. Maybe I am asking them to sit for too long or it is not interesting to them.
	A lot of waiting time	After washing hands, children sit at tables waiting for lunch. They sit for ten minutes.	Children end up waiting a lot during transitions. I try to get them all to obey before we move between activities. I get so frustrated. I need to look for ways to make transitions easier for us all.
Space Design	Spaces too small	Children bump into each other and their structures in the block center.	N/A
	Too much undefined space	Lack of furniture creates lots of room for running or roughhousing.	N/A
Material Options	Too few materials	Children argue over materials because there are not enough interesting choices.	N/A
	Too many choices	Children appear overwhelmed as shelves are overpacked with materials.	N/A
	Inappropriate materials	Materials are either below or above children's developmental levels.	N/A
Teacher Responsiveness		Lesson plans are often unchanging from year to year. Plans do not change in response to children's interests or developmental needs.	My circle times are pretty much the same every day. That would explain why children are not interested. I should look for ways to mix it up a little.
Sensory Stimulation		Classrooms overwhelm one or more of children's senses.	N/A
Temptations		Teacher often says "no." Many parts of the classroom or many materials are off-limits.	N/A
Physical Development Needs		Children are using their large muscles (throwing, hitting, climbing) in inappropriate ways. There are no appropriate opportunities to use these muscles or skills in the classroom.	N/A
Opportunities for Choice and Power		Children have very little free choice time and few opportunities to make choices about the activities in the classroom.	Children don't seem to enjoy the art projects I plan. They try to rush through them, and there are behavior challenges at this time of day. I need to let them decide when and how to use the materials.
Clarity of Expectations		Children appear confused about what the teacher expects of them.	N/A
Presence of Joy		Most of the interactions in the classroom are corrective or negative. There is a lack of laughter and joy.	Transitions are not fun for children or for me. I bet I could make them more fun for all of us.

Figure 8.3 Sample Behavior Documentation Forms: Ashley

Behavior Documentation Form

Child: Ashley R.   **Teacher:** Ms. Noemi   **Date/Time:** November 16, 10:20 a.m.

What happened before the behavior?

It was storytime. Ashley was off her carpet square and touching Aisha's hair. Aisha said, "Teacher, Ashley is touching me."

Where did the behavior occur?

Storytime in library

Description of behavior:

I pointed out to Ashley that she needed to be on her carpet square so she could hear the story and that Aisha told her she did not want Ashley to touch her hair. Ashley laid on her carpet square and began to kick her legs and scream, "I hate story!" When Mr. Jamal approached her, she got up and pushed over a bookshelf near the carpet.

Who was involved in the behavior (children near, teachers present)?

All the children were in the area. No one else was directly involved in the correction other than me and Mr. Jamal.

What feelings did the child appear to exhibit during the behavior?

Ashley appeared distraught and angry at being corrected. She expressed dislike of storytime and upset with the correction from Mr. Jamal.

Behavior Documentation Form

Child: Ashley R.   **Teacher:** Ms. Noemi   **Date/Time:** November 18, 4:45 p.m.

What happened before the behavior?

Ashley was in the block center stacking blocks next to Sang and Bertram, who were putting together a train track. It appears that one of the other children bumped into Ashley, causing her to stumble and knock down her own stack.

Where did the behavior occur?

Block center

Description of behavior:

I heard Ashley swear and Bertram begin to cry. When I went to him, he told me that Ashley had hit him. Ashley screamed, "He bumped me and ruined my building!" When I reminded her that we cannot allow hitting, no matter what, she threw down two blocks and stomped away.

Who was involved in the behavior (children near, teachers present)?

Sang and Bertram

What feelings did the child appear to exhibit during the behavior?

Ashley appeared angry because she felt that someone had done something to her. When Bertram explained what happened, she appeared to feel bad about hitting him. Her use of a swear word appeared to be a response to her surprise and frustration.

Figure 8.3 Sample Behavior Documentation Forms: Ashley (continued)

Behavior Documentation Form

Child: Ashley R.   **Teacher:** Ms. Noemi   **Date/Time:** November 19, 10:30 a.m.

What happened before the behavior?
The class was listening to story. Ashley was not listening and trying to get toys off a nearby shelf.

Where did the behavior occur?
Storytime in library

Description of behavior:
I asked Ashley to put away a toy. She threw the toy and began to run around the classroom laughing. When Mr. Jamal attempted to stop her, she pushed over a chair and jumped on a table.

Who was involved in the behavior (children near, teachers present)?
Mr. Jamal and me

What feelings did the child appear to exhibit during the behavior?
Ashley appeared bored beforehand. When corrected, she at first appeared frustrated, but then appeared amused as she was running around the classroom.

Behavior Documentation Form

Child: Ashley R.   **Teacher:** Ms. Noemi   **Date/Time:** December 7, 11:15 a.m.

What happened before the behavior?
Ashley was playing by herself with the geoboard game.

Where did the behavior occur?
Math & manipulatives center

Description of behavior:
While Ashley was playing with the geoboard game, a rubber band snapped and popped her finger. She said "sh—" very loudly. When other children laughed, she repeated the word twice.

Who was involved in the behavior (children near, teachers present)?
Several children were nearby.

What feelings did the child appear to exhibit during the behavior?
She appeared startled and upset when her finger was hurt. She seemed amused and proud as she noticed other children reacting to her swearing.

Figure 8.3 Sample Behavior Documentation Forms: Ashley (continued)

Behavior Documentation Form

Child: _Ashley R._   Teacher: _Ms. Noemi_   Date/Time: _December 7, 12:50 p.m._

What happened before the behavior?

It was during naptime, and the room was quiet.

Where did the behavior occur?

Classroom

Description of behavior:

During naptime, Ashley loudly blurted out the word "sh—" As Mr. Jamal approached her, she repeated it numerous times. She stopped as he started to rub her back to help her sleep.

Who was involved in the behavior (children near, teachers present)?

Mr. Jamal

What feelings did the child appear to exhibit during the behavior?

I did not notice her feelings before or during, but as Mr. Jamal was rubbing her back, she seemed content and calm.

Behavior Documentation Form

Child: _Ashley R._   Teacher: _Ms. Noemi_   Date/Time: _December 11, 5:15 p.m._

What happened before the behavior?

Ashley was looking out the window and saw her mom pull up outside. Her mom went to pick up Ashley's baby brother in the infant room first.

Where did the behavior occur?

Block center

Description of behavior:

Ashley walked away from the window exclaiming, "My mom is here. Bye Ms. Noemi!" She gathered her coat and belongings and waited by the door. After about 15 minutes of waiting she slammed down her backpack and yelled, "sh—" three times. She fell to the floor crying, and screamed and kicked her legs until her mom came in the room.

Who was involved in the behavior (children near, teachers present)?

Just me

What feelings did the child appear to exhibit during the behavior?

Ashley was excited to see her mom. She was disappointed when she realized that mom had gone to pick up her brother first. She appeared sad as she was having her tantrum.

Figure 8.4 Sample Family-Teacher Conference Form: Ashley and Her Family

Child: Ashley R.   **Date/Time:** December 15

Adults Present: Teachers: Ms. Noemi and Mr. Jamal. Parents: Mom and stepdad. Director: Maya

CHILD'S STRENGTHS	
At home	**At school**
Good helper, likes to help with baby brother	Funny, likes to make people laugh
Sweet, always giving hugs and saying nice things	Good friend, cares deeply about other children
	Physically adept

CHILD'S INTERESTS	
At home	**At school**
Reading and stories	Strong interest in stories and reading
Pretend kitchen	Loves to play superhero

CONCERNING BEHAVIORS	
At home	**At school**
Swearing	Swearing
Clinginess	Reactions to frustration (under control and getting better with current interventions)

PLANS FOR CHILD'S SUCCESS	
At home	**At school**
Mom will carve out one-on-one time with Ashley.	Once a week, Mom will drop brother off first and spend 5 minutes with Ashley in the classroom.
Ignore swearing and give attention to positive behaviors.	Mom will write notes to Ashley. Teachers will read them to her throughout the day.
Be intentional about telling others how helpful and sweet Ashley is (unrelated to brother).	Give as little attention as possible to the swearing and lots of attention to positive behaviors.
	Enlist management to read stories to Ashley once or twice a week.

Local Resources: At this time, we feel there is no need to bring in additional resources or refer the family to other services.

Follow-Up Date: Phone check-ins weekly. We will determine after a few weeks if a follow-up meeting is needed.

Figure 8.5 Sample Plan to Meet Child's Social and Emotional Needs: Ashley

Child: _Ashley R._   **Date/Time:** _December 15_

Adults Present: _Teachers: Ms. Noemi and Mr. Jamal. Parents: Mom and stepdad. Director: Maya_

Child's Behavior	Background Information
Swearing—seen at home and at school	Mom had a baby with her new husband 8 weeks ago. Ashley remained in center during maternity leave. Swearing began the week the brother started attending center. Dad transferred to another state for work and hasn't visited in 4 months.

Child's Possible Emotions	Contextual Cues
Ashley seems to display a range of emotions before, during, and after swearing. We have seen sadness, boredom, frustration, and amusement.	We notice that Ashley seems to look around at others before and after swearing as if to gauge their reactions. She laughs at the reactions. She also is by herself and appears bored before she swears.

Possible Unmet Social-Emotional Need(s):

Need for attention?

PLAN TO MEET NEED(S)		
Environments	**Experiences**	**Relationships**
Move Ashley's cot to front of room, closer to teacher, so it's easier for teacher to rub her back and see the rest of the room.	Small-group activity—making superhero capes to put in the pretend center. Find a time to let Ashley pick a story for literacy circle. Give her a turn in the reader chair. Help Ashley write letters to her dad.	Read notes from Mom when sent in. Once a week, arrange for Mom to call Ashley at school. Mr. Jamal and Ms. Noemi will look for opportunities to spend one-on-one time with Ashley.

Outside Resources: None at this time.

Follow-Up Date: Weekly phone calls as needed.

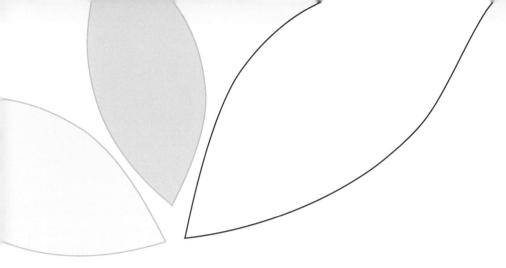

Conclusion:
Appreciate the Beauty of the Harvest

Three years ago, my husband and I hosted a gathering of friends at our home. One friend brought us a beautiful Christmas cactus as a gift. While I appreciated the gesture, I looked at the plant with pity. I suspected that given our skill with plants, it would be dead within a few months. My husband, however, was determined that this plant would not only survive in our home, but thrive.

He went online to research what a Christmas cactus needed. He bought special food and carefully measured out the required water. He moved the plant around the house so that it would get the light it needed according to the season. Today, three years later, the plant sits next to me as I write these words—abloom with lovely flowers.

Imagine if early childhood educators approached children with the same tenacity—confident in their knowledge that each child can and will succeed. When teachers approach their jobs as gardeners, they bring a determination to help each sprout flourish in the complex world in which it lives.

Because of the realities many families face today, a small fraction of children might still be unsuccessful in the classroom setting due to deep unmet social-emotional needs. These children have spent much of their young lives in home situations or educational settings that consistently deny them the basic care and attention they need. However, when teachers use the strategies in this book to shift their focus from "fixing" a child with challenging behavior to creating an environment in which that child is more likely to thrive, more children can succeed. How we approach classroom management and design can send a clear message to children: that each child is *valued*, that each is *worthy* of our efforts and investment, and that we will stand with each of them and work *together* to help them be successful.

As a longtime early childhood educator, I am moved by the words of the great Spanish cellist and conductor Pablo Casals in his autobiography *Joys and Sorrows*.[20]

Each second we live in a new and unique moment of the universe, a moment that never was before and never will be again. And what do we teach our children in school? We teach them that two and two make four and that Paris is the capital of France. When will we also teach them what they are? We should say to each of them: Do you know what you are? You are a marvel. You are unique. In all the world there is no other child exactly like you. In the millions of years that have passed there has never been another child like you. And look at your body—what a wonder it is! Your legs, your arms, your clever fingers, the way you move! You may become a Shakespeare, a Michelangelo, a Beethoven. You have the capacity for anything. Yes, you are a marvel. And when you grow up, can you then harm another who is, like you, a marvel? You must cherish one another. You must work—we all must work—to make this world worthy of its children.

Thank you, readers, for the work you do to make this world worthy of each and every marvel you care for and educate each day.

Notes

Introduction

1. Christina A. Samuels, "Pre-K Suspension Data Prompt Focus on Intervention," *Education Week* 33, no. 27 (March 2014): 6.

2. Walter S. Gilliam, *Prekindergartners Left Behind: Expulsion Rates in State Prekindergarten Programs* (New York: Foundation for Child Development, 2005).

3. United States Department of Education, Office for Civil Rights, *Civil Rights Data Collection: Data Snapshot (Early Childhood)* (Washington, DC: United States Department of Education, 2014).

4. Since the time of my attendance at their institute, the good work of CSEFEL and their pyramid model have transitioned to the Pyramid Model Consortium at pyramidmodel.org.

Chapter 1

5. Marlynn K. Clayton with Mary Beth Forton, *Classroom Spaces That Work* (Turners Falls, MA: Northeast Foundation for Children, 2001); Hatice Zeynep Inan, "The Third Dimension in Preschools: Preschool Environments and Classroom Design," *European Journal of Educational Studies* 1, no. 1 (2009): 55–66; Lilian G. Katz, *Lively Minds: Distinctions Between Academic Versus Intellectual Goals for Young Children* (Jamaica Plain, MA: Defending the Early Years, 2015).

6. David Elkind, *The Hurried Child: Growing Up Too Fast Too Soon* (New York: Perseus Books, 2001).

7. Steve Biddulph, *Raising Boys: Why Boys Are Different—and How to Help Them Become Happy and Well-Balanced Men* (Berkeley, CA: Ten Speed Press, 2013).

8. Reggio Emilia is a student-centered, experiential learning approach founded in Italy in the mid-twentieth century.

9. Jim Greenman, *Caring Spaces, Learning Places: Children's Environments That Work* (Redmond, VA: Exchange Press, 2007).

Chapter 2

10. Elizabeth Baraff Bonawitz et al., "Children Balance Theories and Evidence in Exploration, Explanation, and Learning," *Cognitive Psychology* 64, no. 4 (June 2012): 215–234.

11. Lilian G. Katz, *Lively Minds: Distinctions Between Academic Versus Intellectual Goals for Young Children* (Jamaica Plain, MA: Defending the Early Years, 2015).

12. Alliance for Childhood, "A Call to Action on the Education of Young Children," February 23, 2006, www.allianceforchildhood.org; Lawrence J. Schweinhart et al., *Lifetime Effects: The High/Scope Perry Preschool Study Through Age 40* (Ypsilanti, MI: High/Scope Press, 2005).

13. Richard Louv, *Last Child in the Woods: Saving Our Children from Nature-Deficit Disorder* (Chapel Hill, NC: Algonquin Books, 2005).

14. Jack P. Shonkoff and Deborah A. Phillips (eds.), *From Neurons to Neighborhoods: The Science of Early Childhood Development* (Washington, DC: National Academy Press, 2000).

15. Sallee J. Beneke, Michaelene M. Ostrosky, and Lilian G. Katz, "Calendar Time for Young Children: Good Intentions Gone Awry," *Young Children* 63, no. 3 (May 2008): 12–16.

Chapter 4

16. Alfie Kohn, *Punished by Rewards: The Trouble with Gold Stars, Incentive Plans, A's, Praise, and Other Bribes* (Boston: Houghton Mifflin, 1993).

Chapter 5

17. Carol Garhart Mooney, *Theories of Childhood: An Introduction to Dewey, Montessori, Erikson, Piaget & Vygotsky* (St. Paul, MN: Redleaf Press, 2013).

Chapter 6

18. Jean F. Kelly et al., *Promoting First Relationships: A Program for Service Providers to Help Parents and Other Caregivers Nurture Young Children's Social and Emotional Development* (Seattle, WA: NCAST Programs, 2008). (Available at ncast.org.)

19. Julianne Holt-Lunstad et al., "Loneliness and Social Isolation as Risk Factors for Mortality: A Meta-Analytic Review," *Perspectives of Psychological Science* 10, no. 3 (March 2015): 227–237.

Conclusion

20. Pablo Casals with Albert E. Kahn, *Joys and Sorrows: Reflections by Pablo Casals, As Told to Albert E. Kahn* (New York: Simon & Schuster, 1970).

References and Resources

Alliance for Childhood. "A Call to Action on the Education of Young Children." February 23, 2006. www.allianceforchildhood.org.

Alliance for Childhood. *Crisis in the Kindergarten: Why Children Need to Play in School*. College Park, MD: Alliance for Childhood, 2009.

American Academy of Pediatrics Council on School Health. "Out-of-School Suspension and Expulsion." *Pediatrics* 131, no. 3 (March 2013): 1000–1007.

Beneke, Sallee J., Michaelene M. Ostrosky, and Lilian G. Katz. "Calendar Time for Young Children: Good Intentions Gone Awry." *Young Children* 63, no. 3 (May 2008): 12–16.

Bergen, Doris. "The Role of Pretend Play in Children's Cognitive Development." *Early Childhood Research and Practice* 4, no. 1 (2002): 2–15.

Berk, Laura E., Trisha D. Mann, and Amy T. Ogan. "Make-Believe Play: Wellspring for Development of Self-Regulation." In *Play = Learning: How Play Motivates and Enhances Children's Cognitive and Social-Emotional Growth*, edited by Dorothy G. Singer, Roberta Michnick Golinkoff, and Kathy Hirsh-Pasek, 74–100. New York: Oxford University Press, 2006.

Biddulph, Steve. *Raising Boys: Why Boys Are Different—and How to Help Them Become Happy and Well-Balanced Men*. Berkeley, CA: Ten Speed Press, 2013.

Bodrova, Elena and Deborah J. Leong. *Tools of the Mind: The Vygotskian Approach to Early Childhood Education*. Upper Saddle River, NJ: Pearson, 2007.

Bonawitz, Elizabeth Baraff et al. "Children Balance Theories and Evidence in Exploration, Explanation, and Learning." *Cognitive Psychology* 64, no. 4 (June 2012): 215–234.

Bradshaw, Catherine P., Tracy E. Waasdorp, and Philip J. Leaf. "Effects of School-Wide Positive Behavioral Interventions and Supports on Child Behavior Problems." *Pediatrics* 130, no. 5 (November 2012): 1136–1145.

Buchsbaum, Daphna, et al. "Children's Imitation of Causal Action Sequences Is Influenced by Statistical and Pedagogical Evidence." *Cognition* 120, no. 3 (September 2011): 331–340.

Clayton, Marlynn K. with Mary Beth Forton. *Classroom Spaces That Work*. Turners Falls, MA: Northeast Foundation for Children, 2001.

Curtis, Deb and Margie Carter. *Designs for Living and Learning: Transforming Early Childhood Environments*. St. Paul, MN: Redleaf Press, 2015.

Curtis, Deb et al. "Planning Environments and Materials That Respond to Young Children's Lively Minds." *Young Children* 68, no. 4 (September 2013): 26–31.

DeViney, Jessica et al. *Inspiring Spaces for Young Children*. Silver Spring, MD: Gryphon House, 2010.

Duncan, Sandra and Michelle Salcedo. "Are Your Children in Times Square? Moving from Confinement to Engagement." *Exchange* (January/February 2015): 26–29.

Duncan, Sandra and Michelle Salcedo. "Are Your Children in Times Square? Moving from Sensory Overload to Sensory Engagement." *Exchange* 208 (November 2012): 48–52.

Edwards, Carolyn, Lella Gandini, and George Forman, eds. *The Hundred Languages of Children: The Reggio Emilia Experience in Transformation*. Norwood, NJ: Ablex, 2011.

Elkind, David. *The Hurried Child: Growing Up Too Fast Too Soon*. New York: Perseus Books, 2001.

Elkind, David. *The Power of Play: Learning What Comes Naturally*. Cambridge, MA: Da Capo Press, 2007.

Ethridge, Elizabeth Ann and James R. King. "Calendar Math in Preschool and Primary Classrooms: Questioning the Curriculum." *Early Childhood Education Journal* 32, no. 5 (April 2005): 291–296.

Evans, Betsy. *You Can't Come to My Birthday Party! Conflict Resolution with Young Children*. Ypsilanti, MI: High/Scope Press, 2002.

Ferguson, C.J. "Spanking, Corporal Punishment, and Negative Long-Term Outcomes: A Meta-Analytic Review of Longitudinal Studies." *Clinical Psychology Review* 33, no. 1 (February 2013): 196–208.

Fisher, Anna V., Karrie E. Godwin, and Howard Seltman. "Visual Environment, Attention Allocation, and Learning in Young Children: When Too Much of a Good Thing May Be Bad." *Psychological Science* 25, no. 7 (2014): 1362–1370.

Fox, Lise et al. *Response to Intervention and the Pyramid Model*. Tampa, FL: University of South Florida, Technical Assistance Center on Social Emotional Intervention for Young Children, 2009.

Galinsky, Ellen. *Mind in the Making: The Seven Essential Life Skills Every Child Needs*. New York: HarperCollins, 2010.

Gandini, Lella. "The Story and Foundations of the Reggio Emilia Approach." In *Teaching and Learning: Collaborative Exploration of the Reggio Emilia Approach*, edited by Victoria R. Fu, Andrew J. Stremmel, and Lynn T. Hill. Upper Saddle River, NJ: Pearson, 2001.

Gartrell, Daniel. "Replacing Time-Out: Part One—Using Guidance to Build an Encouraging Classroom." *Young Children* 56, no. 6 (November 2001): 8–16.

Gershoff, Elizabeth. "Corporal Punishment by Parents and Associated Child Behaviors and Experiences: A Meta-Analytic and Theoretical Review." *Psychological Bulletin* 128, no. 4 (2002): 539–579.

Gilliam, Walter S. "Implementing Policies to Reduce the Likelihood of Preschool Expulsion." Foundation for Child Development, FCD Policy Brief Series No. 7 (January 2008).

Gilliam, Walter S. "Prekindergartners Left Behind: Expulsion Rates in State Prekindergarten Programs." Foundation for Child Development, FCD Policy Brief Series No. 3 (May 2005).

Gilliam, Walter S. et al. *Do Early Educators' Implicit Biases Regarding Sex and Race Relate to Behavior Expectations and Recommendations of Preschool Expulsions and Suspensions?* New Haven, CT: Yale Child Study Center, 2016.

Greenman, Jim. *Caring Spaces, Learning Places: Children's Environments That Work*. Redmond, VA: Exchange Press, 2007.

Greenman, Jim. "The Experience of Space: The Pleasure of Place." *Exchange* 155 (January/February 2004): 36–37.

Holt-Lunstad, Julianne et al. "Loneliness and Social Isolation as Risk Factors for Mortality: A Meta-Analytic Review." *Perspectives of Psychological Science* 10, no. 3 (March 2015): 227–237.

Inan, Hatice Zeynep. "The Third Dimension in Preschools: Preschool Environments and Classroom Design," *European Journal of Educational Studies* 1, no. 1 (2009): 55–66

International Reading Association (IRA) and the National Association for the Education of Young Children (NAEYC). "Learning to Read and Write: Developmentally Appropriate Practices for Young Children." *Young Children* 53, no. 4 (May 1998): 30–46.

Jacobson, Linda. "Preschoolers Expelled from School at Rates Exceeding That of K–12." *Education Week* 24, no. 37 (May 2005): 1, 12.

Katz, Lilian G. *Lively Minds: Distinctions Between Academic Versus Intellectual Goals for Young Children*. Jamaica Plain, MA: Defending the Early Years, 2015.

Katz, Lilian G., Sylvia C. Chard, and Yvonne Kogan. *Engaging Children's Minds: The Project Approach*. Santa Barbara, CA: Praeger, 2014.

Kelly, Jean F. et al. *Promoting First Relationships: A Program for Service Providers to Help Parents and Other Caregivers Nurture Young Children's Social and Emotional Development*. Seattle, WA: NCAST Programs, 2008.

Kohli, Rita and Daniel G. Solórzano. "Teachers, Please Learn Our Names! Racial Microagressions and the K–12 Classroom." *Race, Ethnicity, and Education* 15, no. 4 (2012): 441–462.

Kohn, Alfie. *Punished by Rewards: The Trouble with Gold Stars, Incentive Plans, A's, Praise, and Other Bribes*. Boston: Houghton Mifflin, 1993.

Louv, Richard. *Last Child in the Woods: Saving Our Children from Nature-Deficit Disorder*. Chapel Hill, NC: Algonquin Books, 2008.

Mooney, Carol Garhart. *Theories of Childhood: An Introduction to Dewey, Montessori, Erikson, Piaget & Vygotsky*. St. Paul, MN: Redleaf Press, 2013.

National Association for the Education of Young Children (NAEYC). *Standing Together Against Suspension & Expulsion in Early Childhood: A Joint Statement*. Washington, DC: NAEYC, 2016. Retrieved from www.naeyc.org.

National Association for the Education of Young Children (NAEYC) and the National Association of Early Childhood Specialists in State Departments of Education (NAECS/SDE). *Early Childhood Curriculum, Assessment, and Program Evaluation: Building an Effective, Accountable System in Programs for Children Birth Through Age 8*. Washington, DC: NAEYC, 2003. Retrieved from www.naeyc.org.

National Scientific Council on the Developing Child. *The Science of Early Childhood Development: Closing the Gap Between What We Know and What We Do*. Cambridge, MA: National Scientific Council on the Developing Child, 2007.

Neuman, Susan B. "The Knowledge Gap: Implications for Early Education." In *Handbook of Early Literacy Research*, edited by Susan B. Neuman and David K. Dickinson. New York: Guilford, forthcoming.

Neuman, Susan B., Carol Copple, and Sue Bredekamp. *Learning to Read and Write: Developmentally Appropriate Practices for Young Children*. Washington, DC: NAEYC, 2000.

Neuman, Susan B. and Kathy Roskos. "Access to Print for Children of Poverty: Differential Effects of Adult Mediation and Literacy-Enriched Play Settings on Environmental and Functional Print Tasks." *American Educational Research Journal* 30, no. 3 (March 1993): 95–122.

Neuman, Susan B. and Kathy Roskos. "Literacy Objects as Cultural Tools: Effects on Children's Literacy Behaviors in Play." *Reading Research Quarterly* 27, no. 3 (Summer 1992): 202–225.

Pellegrini, Anthony D. "Research and Policy on Children's Play." *Child Development Perspectives* 3, no. 2 (August 2009): 131–136.

Piaget, Jean. *The Origins of Intelligence in Children*. Guilford, CT: International Universities Press, 1992.

Salcedo, Michelle. "Classrooms as the Root of Challenging Behaviors." *Exchange* 231 (September/October 2016): 24–28.

Samuels, Christina A. "Pre-K Suspension Data Prompt Focus on Intervention." *Education Week* 33, no. 27 (March 2014): 6.

Schickedanz, Judith A. and Renée M. Casbergue. *Writing in Preschool: Learning to Orchestrate Meaning and Marks*. Newark, DE: International Reading Association, 2009.

Schore, Allan N. "Effects of a Secure Attachment Relationship on Right Brain Development, Affect Regulation, and Infant Mental Health." *Infant Mental Health Journal* 22 (2001): 7–66.

Schweinhart, Lawrence J. et al. *Lifetime Effects: The High/Scope Perry Preschool Study Through Age 40*. Ypsilanti, MI: High/Scope Press, 2005.

Shield, Bridget M. and Julie E. Dockrell. "The Effects of Environmental and Classroom Noise on the Academic Attainments of Primary School Children." *The Journal of the Acoustical Society of America* 123, no. 1 (January 2008): 133–144.

Shonkoff, Jack P. and Deborah A. Phillips, eds. *From Neurons to Neighborhoods: The Science of Early Childhood Development*. Washington, DC: National Academy Press, 2000.

Singer, Dorothy G. et al. "A Role for Play in the Preschool Curriculum." In *All Work and No Play: How Educational Reforms Are Harming Our Preschoolers*, edited by Sharna Olfman. Westport, CT: Praeger, 2003.

Smilansky, Sara. "Sociodramatic Play: Its Relevance to Behavior and Achievement in School." In *Children's Play and Learning: Perspectives and Policy Implications*, edited by Edgar Klugman and Sara Smilansky. New York: Teachers College Press, 1990.

United States Department of Education, Office for Civil Rights. *Civil Rights Data Collection: Data Snapshot (Early Childhood)*. Washington, DC: United States Department of Education, 2014.

Wood, Kay C., Harlan Smith, and Daurice Grossniklaus. "Piaget's Stages." In *Emerging Perspectives on Learning, Teaching, and Technology*, edited by Michael Orey. Athens, GA: University of Georgia, 2010.

Wurm, Julianne P. *Working in the Reggio Way: A Beginner's Guide for American Teachers*. St. Paul, MN: Redleaf Press, 2005.

Zigler, Edward F., Dorothy G. Singer, and Sandra J. Bishop-Josef, eds. *Children's Play: The Roots of Reading*. Washington, DC: Zero to Three Press, 2004.

Appendix

HOMES Active Learning Scale

Activity:

H Hands-on			O Open-ended			M Meaningful			E Engaging			S Sensory-oriented			
Are children interacting with real materials? Does the activity involve them doing something?			Does the activity allow children to explore or is there a predetermined outcome?			Does the activity connect to children's experiences or interests?			Does the activity create opportunities for children to think?			Are there interesting things for children to see, hear, smell, touch, and/or taste?			
0	½	1	0	½	1	0	½	1	0	½	1	0	½	1	Total Points:

What can I do to make this experience more active?

Notes for next time I do this activity:

Classroom Factors Observation Form

CLASSROOM FACTOR	CLASSROOM EXAMPLE	OBSERVATION NOTES
Appropriateness of Expectations	Too high expectations for self-control	Teacher expects that children stand in a straight line before they go outside.	
	A lot of waiting time	After washing hands, children sit at tables waiting for lunch. They sit for ten minutes.	
Space Design	Spaces too small	Children bump into each other and their structures in the block center.	
	Too much undefined space	Lack of furniture creates lots of room for running or roughhousing.	
Material Options	Too few materials	Children argue over materials because there are not enough interesting choices.	
	Too many choices	Children appear overwhelmed as shelves are overpacked with materials.	
	Inappropriate materials	Materials are either below or above children's developmental levels.	

→

Classroom Factors Observation Form (continued)

CLASSROOM FACTOR	CLASSROOM EXAMPLE	OBSERVATION NOTES
Teacher Responsiveness	Lesson plans are often unchanging from year to year. Plans do not change in response to children's interests or developmental needs.	
Sensory Stimulation	Classrooms overwhelm one or more of children's senses.	
Temptations	Teacher often says "no." Many parts of classroom or many materials are off-limits.	
Physical Development Needs	Children are using their large muscles (throwing, hitting, climbing) in inappropriate ways. There are no appropriate opportunities to use these muscles or skills in the classroom.	
Opportunities for Choice and Power	Children have very little free choice time and few opportunities to make choices about the activities in the classroom.	
Clarity of Expectations	Children appear confused about what the teacher expects of them.	
Presence of Joy	Most of the interactions in the classroom are corrective or negative. There is a lack of laughter and joy.	

Strategies for Addressing Challenging Behaviors Throughout the Day

TIME OF DAY	PROACTIVE STRATEGIES	SUPPORTIVE STRATEGIES
Circle Time	Incorporate tenets of active learning so children are involved and engaged. Avoid placing children in passive learner roles. Hold two or three short circle times instead of a single long one. Remove those components (calendar, weather) that add minutes but not substance. Make participation optional. Allow children to participate in a way that meets their learning style (sitting on floor or chair, standing, pacing, lying down). Plan no more than 5 to 7 minutes without movement of some sort. Reflect children's interests.	Provide sensory balls and lap toys for those who want to participate but struggle with keeping hands to themselves. If children start to lose interest, change gears or cut it short. Place children who need additional support near a teacher. If space is limited, provide guidance on how children can use the space safely and comfortably. For example, carpet squares (children can sit on them or stand on them), tape marks that show children a border they must stay within if they are sitting or lying down, and so on.
Cleanup Time	At the start of the year, host a circle time in each center and help children understand how to use it and how to clean it up. Give notice before cleanup time so that children have a chance to finish up what they are doing. Make a cleanup book that explains what is expected during the time. Help children understand why it is important to clean up the room. Use an upbeat and fun cleanup song (I use "I Will Survive" by Gloria Gaynor). Use games during cleanup time: • Hand out cards with pictures of classroom items so children know what to put away. As they finish, they get another card until all cards are gone. • Have children sit in a circle. Select three children to go pick up three items as quickly as possible. When finished, they return and tag another child to go next. Continue until the room is clean. • Play music, name a color, and tell children to pick up all items of that color until you pause the music and say "freeze." Start the music again and name another color. • Invite all children to join you in making a train. As you move from center to center, name a couple of children to clean up the area and rejoin the train as quickly as possible.	Partner with children who struggle during this time. Coach them on their efforts. If children are struggling with a task, leave things where they are and go outside. Clean up after you come back in. If cleanup time is especially challenging for a child, pair her with a child who can help. Provide the child with an alternate activity to do during cleanup time. (If a child is very disruptive, it is more important to meet your goal of cleaning the room and moving children to the next activity than it is to get her to comply.) Give the child very specific tasks that are manageable and easy to understand. For example, "Can you please put those four books on the shelf?" Thank the child and celebrate her success when she meets the goal. At times, you may need to remove the child from a situation before she acts out. A member of management might take the child to help with a task outside the classroom. Because she is removed *before* there is a behavioral issue, the child is not being rewarded for bad behavior, simply provided with an alternative opportunity to be successful. Toward the end of cleanup time, this staff member may return the child to the classroom and help her join in.

Strategies for Addressing Challenging Behaviors Throughout the Day (continued)

TIME OF DAY	PROACTIVE STRATEGIES	SUPPORTIVE STRATEGIES
Naptime	Set up children for success by communicating expectations for naptime. Make a class book telling children what to expect. Make children as comfortable as possible. Invite them to bring in special stuffed toys to sleep with. Walk around and tuck children in and wish them sweet dreams. Play restful music at a low volume so children have to be quiet to hear it. Start nap with a story. Read it aloud in a gentle voice once children are on their cots.	Ask the family to send a special toy with the child that he can only have when he is on his cot. Spend time helping the child calm down. This may include rocking him for a couple of minutes or rubbing his back. If possible, remove a struggling child from the classroom as the teacher focuses on helping other children transition into naptime. Once the others are calm, the struggling child may return to the room and the teacher can give the child her total focus. If a child does not sleep, have a box of special quiet toys that he can use only if he is not bothering children who are sleeping. Have tasks that the child can help with if he is quiet. These may include wiping tables, sorting toys, or drying toys a teacher washes.
Mealtime	Ensure that children understand the expectations for eating in the classroom. Make a picture book to read with children. Serve meals family-style. When children serve themselves, they are more likely to eat what is on their plates. Sit with children and talk with them while they eat. Make mealtimes a pleasant time to chat with each other. Model your expectations. If children must sit and eat, make sure that teachers do not walk around while eating. Create placemats and let children place their mats on the table as part of setting up for meals. This can help children define their space. Avoid power struggles around meals. Unless there is a medical issue, don't worry about how much children eat. Insisting that children "clean their plates" can lead to challenging behaviors. Encourage children to try everything, but don't insist on it.	Sit next to children who are struggling with mealtime. Coach their efforts as they learn the expectations. Set up opportunities to practice these skills in pretend play situations and invite struggling children to participate. For example, set up a restaurant in the pretend play center, have an imaginary picnic outside, or collect examples of silverware to sort in the math center (talk about how you use these implements as you sort). Have a conversation with the child's family to understand the behaviors. For example, maybe she eats from other's plates because the family eats from one communal dish at home. Give her a chance to share her traditions with the class. Before meals, remind her how school is different from home. Create a song that you can teach children. Sing the song with children as you wash hands before lunch. Look for opportunities to acknowledge when you see the child meeting behavioral expectations.
Transitions	Limit the number of transitions you have during the day. Give children notice when transitions are going to occur. Be consistent in how the day flows in the classroom. Have a pictorial schedule that reflects the flow and is posted at children's eye level.	Create individual pictorial schedules for children who struggle with transitions. You might arrange pictures together on a clipboard to show how the child's day is going to play out. Partner children who struggle with a teacher during transitions. The teacher might hold the child's hand, give verbal cues about what to do next, or just pay special attention to and affirm the child's efforts.

Strategies for Addressing Challenging Behaviors Throughout the Day (continued)

TIME OF DAY	PROACTIVE STRATEGIES	SUPPORTIVE STRATEGIES
Transitions (continued)	Give children notice when things will be different. Plan for transitions and make them fun using music or silly movements. Place the focus on getting to the next place or time as efficiently as possible, as opposed to getting children to follow directions (such as standing in a straight line or being quiet). Split children into two small groups (each with one teacher) to move between activities instead of trying to move one large group of children. Have visual or auditory cues that let children know what is expected (music for different times of day or placards that tell children what they should be doing).	Involve a child in making decisions about transitions. (Ask, "What song should we sing?" or, "How should we move to the playground?")
Arrival	Have classroom centers open the minute children arrive. If this is not possible, have engaging choices available. Welcome each child and family as they arrive. Have a ritual when children arrive. This may include moving their picture from a home board to a school board or asking them a question of the day. Encourage families to help their children transition into a center before leaving. Encourage families and children to have good-bye rituals. These may include placing kisses on a child's hand that he can store in his pocket for later, when needed. Or giving three hugs and a wave through a window. Discourage adults from sneaking out to avoid upsetting a child. This often makes it harder in the long run, as the child may learn not to trust the adults in his life and might become clingy and afraid to let the adult out of his sight.	Acknowledge a child's feelings if he is struggling. Provide comfort in a way that is meaningful to that child (comforting words, a hug, a quiet space with a book). Ask families to leave something for the child to hold until they return. This could be a pretend credit or ID card or key. Sometimes children feel more secure if they believe their parent needs to return to get that item. Use a pictorial schedule to help children know when to expect a family member to return. Invite families to leave notes that a teacher can read to the child throughout the day.
End of Day	Have classroom centers open until the last child leaves. If this is not possible, have engaging materials or activities available to children. Take advantage of times when there are only a few children to spend one-on-one time with them (instead of cleaning up or doing closing tasks).	Create rituals with a child who is consistently the last one to be picked up. For example, maybe you share a special story together or play a favorite game. Have some of the child's favorite materials put away in a container. Bring out the materials when most other children are gone to make the end of the day special for her. Involve children in the end-of-the-day procedures. They can help wipe tables, sort toys, or find materials for the following day.

Behavior Documentation Form

Child: _____ Teacher: _____ Date/Time: _____

What happened before the behavior?	Where did the behavior occur?

Description of behavior:

Who was involved in the behavior (children near, teachers present)?	What feelings did the child appear to exhibit during the behavior?

What I Need: A Child's List of Social and Emotional Needs

Even though I may look small, I have the same social-emotional needs as all human beings. When the adults in my life meet these needs consistently, I am better able to learn and develop.

To be safe and secure.
I need to know that I am physically and emotionally safe. I need to trust that the adults in my life will work to guard me from dangers, to protect my feelings, and not to put me in situations in which I cannot succeed.

To be loved and have a sense of self-worth.
I need to know that someone thinks I am the center of the universe. I need to believe that there is an adult in this world who will go to the ends of the earth to show me I matter.

To receive attention and be understood.
I need to know that someone is paying attention to me. I need to expect that someone values what I have to say and takes joy in what I do.

To have a sense of control and predictability.
I need to feel like I have some control in my life. I need adults in my life who are predictable in their behaviors and who structure my day with predictable routines and rituals.

To recognize and be able to handle strong feelings.
I need to know that the emotions that overwhelm me sometimes are normal. I need the adults around me to remain calm in the face of my feelings, to help me give them a name, and to provide me with safe and healthy ways to express them.

To have a sense of power and feel independent and competent.
I need to feel powerful sometimes. I build this sense of power when I am given choices, when I am presented with tasks at which I can succeed (sometimes with a little help), and when the adults around me notice what I do well.

To be engaged in stimulating pursuits.
I need to experience the world. My brain develops as I am presented with interesting materials to see, touch, hear, smell, and taste.

To enjoy relationships and have a sense of belonging.
I need to know that if I were not on this earth, someone would miss me. I need to feel like someone is glad that I am his or her companion and that I can count on him or her always being mine.

Getting to Know You: A Family Survey

We are committed to creating a classroom experience that celebrates you, your child, and your family. Thank you for taking the time to fill out this survey and help us get to know you a little better.

Your Child:

1. When you think about your child's future, what do you want for him/her?

2. Describe your child's personality (moods, temperament, likes, dislikes, how your child communicates, and so on).

3. Does your child have a nickname that you and other family members use?

4. Tell us about your child's sleeping patterns. How does he/she go to sleep?

5. Tell us about your child's eating habits. What are his/her favorite foods?

6. Does your child have any special comfort items (blanket, stuffed animal)?

Getting to Know You: A Family Survey (continued)

Your Family:

7. What are your family's hobbies and interests? What do you like to do together?

8. How does your family eat dinner? What are your favorite meals?

9. Tell us about the holidays your family celebrates. What traditions do you have?

10. How do you celebrate birthdays in your family?

11. Who is involved with your child on a regular basis (extended family, friends)?

12. What makes your family special?

Family-Teacher Conference Form

Child's Name: _____ Adults Present: _____ Date/Time: _____

CHILD'S STRENGTHS	
At home	**At school**

CHILD'S INTERESTS	
At home	**At school**

CONCERNING BEHAVIORS	
At home	**At school**

→

Family-Teacher Conference Form (continued)

PLANS FOR CHILD'S SUCCESS	
At home	At school

Local Resources:

Follow-Up Date: _____

Teacher Signature: _____

Director Signature: _____

Parent Signature: _____

Plan to Meet Child's Social and Emotional Needs

Child's Name: _____ Adults Present: _____ Date: _____

Child's Behavior	Background Information
Child's Possible Emotions	**Contextual Cues**

Possible Unmet Social-Emotional Need(s):

PLAN TO MEET NEED(S)		
Environments	Experiences	Relationships

Outside Resources:

Follow-Up Date: _____

Teacher Signature: _____

Director Signature: _____

Parent Signature: _____

Index

About the Author

Michelle Salcedo, M.Ed., has worked in the field of early childhood for over thirty years, starting as a teacher's helper in her younger brother's center. She has served as a teacher, director, trainer, and family educator in numerous childcare settings across Michigan, South Carolina, and Spain. Michelle has led the education initiatives of two of the largest childcare firms in the United States. Her articles on young children frequently appear in various electronic and print publications and she has traveled the country speaking at local, state, and national conferences. Currently she is a content developer for a national early childhood training company. Michelle lives in Greenville, South Carolina.

Photo by Whitney Barnard

Contact Michelle at **michellesalcedo.com**.